CLASSIC SERMONS ON LESSER-KNOWN BIBLE CHARACTERS

The Kregel Classic Sermons Series

Angels
Apostle Paul
Apostle Peter
Attributes of God
Birth of Christ
Christian Service
Church
Cross of Christ
Death and Dying
Faith and Doubt
Family and Home
Grace of God
Heaven and Hell
Holy Spirit
Hope
Judas Iscariot
Lesser-Known Bible Characters
Lord's Prayer
Love of God
Miracles of Jesus
Names of God
Old Testament Prophets
Overcoming Fear
Parables of Jesus
Praise
Prayer
Prodigal Son
Resurrection of Christ
Revival and Spiritual Renewal
Seasons of Life
Second Coming/Prophetic Themes
Sovereignty of God
Spiritual Warfare
Stewardship
Suffering
Will of God
Word of God
World Evangelism
Worship

KREGEL CLASSIC SERMONS SERIES

CLASSIC SERMONS ON LESSER-KNOWN BIBLE CHARACTERS

Compiled by
Warren W. Wiersbe

Grand Rapids, MI 49501

Classic Sermons on Lesser-Known Bible Characters
Compiled by Warren W. Wiersbe

© 2000 by Kregel Publications. All rights reserved. No part of this book may be reproduced, stored in a retrieval system, or transmitted in any form or by any means—electronic, mechanical, photocopy, recording, or otherwise—without written permission of the publisher, except for brief quotations in printed reviews.

Published by Kregel Publications, a division of Kregel, Inc., P.O. Box 2607, Grand Rapids, MI 49501. Kregel Publications provides trusted, biblical publications for Christian growth and service. Your comments and suggestions are valued.

Scripture used by permission of Thomas Nelson, Inc., original publisher of the American Standard Version.

For more information about Kregel Publications, visit our web site at: www.kregel.com

Cover photo: PhotoDisc

Library of Congress Cataloging-in-Publication Data
Classic sermons on lesser-known Bible characters / Warren W. Wiersbe, compiler.
    p.   cm.— (Kregel classic sermons series)

ISBN 0-8254-4151-x

Printed in the United States of America
1 2 3 4 5 / 04 03 02 01 00

Contents

List of Scripture Texts 6
Preface 7
1. Micaiah: In Prison for Conscience' Sake 9
   Clarence Edward Noble Macartney
2. Mnason: An Old Disciple 19
   Alexander Maclaren
3. Malchus: To Christ for Healing Love 29
   Walter A. Maier
4. Caleb: An Old Testament Good Man 43
   George W. Truett
5. Jeroboam's Wife: A Hearer in Disguise 57
   Charles Haddon Spurgeon
6. Enoch: Walking with God 77
   George H. Morrison
7. Simon Magus 85
   Alexander Whyte
8. Esau: The Profane 95
   George Campbell Morgan
9. Hobab: The Slave of the Second Best 109
   Clovis Gillham Chappell
10. Judas (Not Iscariot) 119
    John Daniel Jones
11. Onesiphorus: A Friend in Chains 131
    Clarence Edward Noble Macartney
12. Simon of Cyrene: Up from the Country and
    Pressed into the Service 141
    Charles Haddon Spurgeon

5

List of Scripture Texts

Genesis 5:22, Morrison 77
Genesis 25:27–34, Morgan 95
Numbers 10:29–31, Chappell 109
Joshua 14:6, Truett 43
1 Kings 14:6, Spurgeon 57
1 Kings 22:8, Macartney 9
Mark 15:21, Spurgeon 141
Luke 22:51, Maier 29
John 14:22, Jones 119
Acts 8:9–25, Whyte 85
Acts 21:16, Maclaren 19
1 Corinthians 1:1–2, Morgan 95
1 Corinthians 3:16–18, Morgan 95
1 Corinthians 6:19–20, Morgan 95
2 Timothy 1:16, Macartney 131
Hebrews 12:16, Morgan 95

Preface

THE *Kregel Classic Sermons Series* is an attempt to assemble and publish meaningful sermons from master preachers about significant themes.

These are *sermons*, not essays or chapters taken from books about themes. Not all of these sermons could be called great, but all of them are *meaningful*. They apply the truths of the Bible to the needs of the human heart, which is something that all effective preaching must do.

While some are better known than others, all of the preachers whose sermons I have selected had important ministries and were highly respected in their day. The fact that a sermon is included in this volume does not mean that either the compiler or the publisher agrees with or endorses everything that the man did, preached, or wrote. The sermon is here because it has a valued contribution to make.

These are sermons about *significant* themes. The pulpit is no place to play with trivia. The preacher has thirty minutes in which to help mend broken hearts, change defeated lives, and save lost souls; he can never accomplish this demanding ministry by distributing homiletical tidbits. In these difficult days we do not need clever pulpiteers who discuss the times; we need dedicated ambassadors who will preach the eternities.

The reading of these sermons can enrich your spiritual life. The studying of them can enrich your skills as an interpreter and expounder of God's truth. However God uses these sermons in your life and ministry, my prayer is that His church around the world will be encouraged and strengthened by them.

—WARREN W. WIERSBE

Micaiah: In Prison for Conscience' Sake

Clarence Edward Noble Macartney (1879–1957) ministered in Paterson, New Jersey, and Philadelphia, Pennsylvania, before assuming the influential pastorate of First Presbyterian Church, Pittsburgh, Pennsylvania, where he ministered for twenty-seven years. His preaching especially attracted men, not only to the Sunday services but also to his popular Tuesday noon luncheons. He was gifted in dealing with Bible biographies and, in this respect, has been called "the American Alexander Whyte." Much of his preaching was topical-textual, but it was always biblical, doctrinal, and practical. Perhaps his most famous sermon is "Come Before Winter."

This sermon selection was taken from *The Wisest Fool and Other Men of the Bible,* published in 1945 by Abingdon-Cokesbury Press.

CLARENCE EDWARD NOBLE MACARTNEY

1

Micaiah: In Prison for Conscience' Sake

There is yet one man, . . . but I hate him. (1 Kings 22:8)

WE ALL HAVE THAT "one man" within our breast, and the natural man hates him, just as Ahab, the king of Israel, hated Micaiah, the fearless prophet of the Lord.

Jehoshaphat, the good king of Judah, had gone down to visit Ahab, the wicked king of Israel, at Samaria. Ahab gave him a great reception and banquet and killed sheep and oxen for him in abundance and for the people that were with him. At this banquet Ahab proposed to Jehoshaphat that they go up and attack the stronghold of Ramoth-gilead, which was still occupied by their inveterate enemies the Syrians. Flattered with the honors paid him by Ahab, Jehoshaphat—whose inclinations generally were Godward, but who on more than one occasion was led astray by wrong associations—said to Ahab that he would go with him on this expedition: "I am as thou art, my people as thy people, my horses as thy horses" (1 Kings 22:4). In other words, Jehoshaphat pledged all the resources of his kingdom to this war against Ramoth-gilead and Syria.

But Jehoshaphat, who was a godly man, did not wish to start upon such an expedition without first inquiring of the Lord. So he said to Ahab, "Inquire, I pray thee, at the word of the

LORD" (v. 5). In answer to this the king of Israel gathered together four hundred of his prophets, or so-called prophets, all of whom made it their business not to declare the word of the Lord, but to tell Ahab to do whatever he wanted to do. These four hundred prophets appeared in the throne room of Ahab's ivory palace at Samaria. The two kings were seated on two thrones, each one of them resplendent with his crown upon his head and crimson and purple robes upon his body. The king of Israel then inquired of the four hundred, saying, "Shall I go against Ramoth-gilead to battle, or shall I forbear?" (v. 6). With one voice these false prophets said, "Go up; for the Lord shall deliver it into the hand of the king" (v. 6).

Jehoshaphat, the king of Judah, apparently was a little disturbed at this quick shout of unanimous approval. He probably did not like the looks of these false prophets. So he said to the king of Israel, "Is there not here a prophet of the LORD besides, that we might inquire of him?" (v. 7). Ahab answered, "There is yet one man, Micaiah the son of Imlah, by whom we may inquire of the LORD: but I hate him; for he doth not prophesy good concerning me, but evil" (v. 8). But Jehoshaphat insisted that this prophet of the Lord be called in. A messenger was then dispatched to summon Micaiah.

In the meantime, one of the false prophets, Zedekiah, put on a bit of acting or show to impress Ahab. He fastened horns of iron on his head and, appearing before the thrones of the two kings, said, "Thus saith the LORD, With these shalt thou push the Syrians, until thou have consumed them" (v. 11). Then all the four hundred shouted together, "Go up to Ramoth-gilead, and prosper: for the LORD shall deliver it into the king's hand" (v. 12).

When the messenger arrived at the house of Micaiah to summon him before the kings, he said to him in effect, "All the other prophets, the four hundred, have told Ahab that if he goes up against Ramoth-gilead he will be victorious. As a friend I would advise you, when you appear before the king, to say the same thing" (see v. 13). But this messenger knew not with whom he was speaking, for Micaiah answered immediately, "As the LORD liveth, what the LORD saith unto me, that will I speak" (v. 14).

Micaiah was brought before Ahab and Jehoshaphat. There he stood, one against four hundred. The two kings, resplendent in their robes and diadems, looked down upon him. Zedekiah, with the iron horns in his hands, stood near, looking scornfully upon Micaiah, and in the great hall the four hundred were silent as they waited to see what Micaiah would say.

Then Ahab addressed the fearless prophet and said: "Shall we go against Ramoth-gilead to battle, or shall we forbear?" (v. 15).

Micaiah answered, "Go, and prosper: for the LORD shall deliver it into the hand of the king" (v. 15). He was speaking, of course, ironically. Ahab's conscience let him know at once that God did not approve the expedition against Ramoth-gilead. As Elijah mocked and defied the false prophets of this same king, so Micaiah mocked them by telling Ahab to go up against Ramoth-gilead and prosper.

The angry king, seeing that Micaiah was mocking him, said to the prophet, "How many times shall I adjure thee that thou tell me nothing but that which is true in the name of the LORD?" (v. 16).

Then Micaiah told him the truth. He gave it in the form of a vision: "I saw all Israel scattered upon the hills, as sheep that have not a shepherd: and the LORD said, These have no master: let them return every man to his house in peace" (v. 17). This vision was a prediction of the defeat and overthrow of Israel in the coming battle, and the calamity which would come upon the nation because it would have no shepherd and king.

Angry and out of sorts, the king of Israel exclaimed to Jehoshaphat, "Did I not tell thee that he would prophesy no good concerning me?" (v. 18). Then Micaiah continued his speech and told of another vision. At a conclave in heaven, with all the host of heaven present, God asked, "Who shall persuade Ahab, that he may go up and fall at Ramoth-gilead?" (v. 20). One suggested this plan and one suggested another plan. Then "there came forth a spirit and stood before the LORD and said, I will persuade him" (v. 21). And God said, "Wherewith?" (v. 22). The spirit answered, "I will go forth, and I will be a lying spirit in the mouth of all his prophets" (v. 22). Micaiah said to Ahab, "The LORD hath put a lying spirit in the mouth of all these thy prophets, and the LORD hath spoken evil concerning thee" (v. 23).

That was a magnificent stand for conscience and truth that Micaiah made, one against four hundred. The immediate consequence was that he was smitten in the face by the leader of the false prophets, Zedekiah, and cast into prison by the king, who told the jailer to "feed him with bread of affliction and with water of affliction" (v. 27). But the name of Micaiah lives forever because of his fidelity to conscience and the Word of God.

Two Truths About Conscience

There are two great truths about conscience that are brought out in this stirring narrative. The first is that, as Luther said at the Diet of Worms when he was asked to recant and deny what he had written and taught in his books, "It is neither safe nor wise to do anything against conscience." Ahab found that out. He was always fighting against his conscience, and always his conscience was overcoming him. When he met Elijah at the time of the great drought that had come down upon Israel because of the king's wickedness, he cried out, "Hast thou found me, O mine enemy?" (21:20). Elijah, as the incarnation of conscience, had indeed found him. Here Ahab called conscience, in the person of the fearless and incorruptible Micaiah, his enemy. When Jehoshaphat asked if there was not yet a prophet of the Lord of whom they could inquire, Ahab answered, "There is yet one man, . . . but I hate him." Conscience always stands in the way of Ramoth-gilead expeditions. Four hundred voices may tell you to go forward and do what you want to do, and only one voice will say to you not to go, that the expedition will end in disaster and judgment and death.

That was what happened to Ahab. He heeded the voice of the four hundred false prophets and cast the one true prophet into prison. So men cast their conscience into prison. He summoned his captains and his army, and together with Jehoshaphat, who probably was somewhat reluctant to go, marched up against Ramoth-gilead. In the great battle that followed, Ahab, when he heard the blare of the trumpets and saw the sun flashing on the helmets and shields and chariots of the Syrian host, remembered very clearly the word of Micaiah warning him not to go. Now the voice of conscience was speaking louder than all those four hundred false prophets. Ahab thought that perhaps he could escape death in the battle by disguising himself as a private soldier. This he did, putting off his royal robes and wearing the armor of a common soldier. But there is no disguise that judgment and retribution cannot penetrate. Jehoshaphat, however, was wearing his royal robes. The king of Syria had commanded his captains to fight neither with small nor great, save only with the king of Israel. Ahab was the man he wanted to kill. At first the captains pursued Jehoshaphat in his chariot, still wearing his royal robes, thinking he was Ahab. But when they learned that he was the king of Judah and not the king of Israel, they turned back from pursuing him.

It looked as if in the rout of the battle Ahab was going to escape. But no! A certain man drew a bow at a venture. The hand of God was on that bow. "A certain man drew a bow at a venture, and smote the king of Israel between the joints of the harness" (22:34). Until the sun went down Ahab was stayed up in his chariot against the Syrians, but in the evening he died. His chariot was then driven back to Samaria. Some of his officers took the chariot down to the pool of Samaria to wash out the blood that had stained it, and as they did so the dogs came and licked up his blood, the very dogs that had licked up the blood of Naboth, whom Ahab had slain that he might take his vineyard, thus fulfilling the prophecy of Elijah: "In the place where dogs licked the blood of Naboth shall dogs lick thy blood, even thine" (21:19). No, it is never safe and never wise to do anything against conscience. In the end, conscience is the victor and the judge.

The Grandeur of Obeying Conscience

If Ahab's history and death show the folly of disobeying and wronging conscience, the history of Micaiah shows the grandeur of obedience to conscience. In the witness that he made to God and the truth, Micaiah was faithful to conscience and the word of God in spite of the majority, the four hundred, who gave a different counsel to the king. He was faithful to conscience in spite of the insults and ridicule that were heaped upon him. He was faithful to conscience although it meant the loss of preferment at the court. He was faithful to conscience although it meant the darkness of the dungeon. But in the dungeon he had that lamp and candle which no wind of evil or human tyranny can ever extinguish—the answer of a good conscience.

When Hugh Latimer, the great reformer of the sixteenth century in England, was preaching one day before Henry VIII, he offended the king by some plain speaking in his sermon. The king ordered him to preach again the next Sunday and to make apology for the offense he had given. On the next Sunday, after he had given out his text, Latimer began by addressing his own soul: "Hugh Latimer, dost thou know before whom thou art this day to speak? To the high and mighty monarch, the king's most excellent majesty, who can take away thy life if thou offendest. Therefore take heed that thou speakest not a word that may displease. But then, consider well, Hugh. Dost thou not know from whence thou comest, upon whose message thou art sent? Even by the great and mighty God, who is all present, and who beholdest all thy ways, and who is able to cast thy soul into hell? Therefore take care that thou deliverest thy message faithfully." He then repeated the sermon he had preached to the king the Sunday before. All in the court were full of expectation to know what the fate of this bold preacher would be. That night the king summoned him, and, in a stern voice, asked him how he could be so bold as to preach to the king in that manner. Latimer replied that he had merely discharged his duty and obeyed his conscience. Upon which the king arose from his seat and, taking the good man by the hand, embraced him saying, "Blessed be God I have so honest a servant." This was the same Latimer who was burned at the stake at Smithfield in the reign of Bloody Mary. In his dying hour he tasted the victory, the thrill of moral victory, for he greeted his fellow martyr Ridley with the famous words, "Be of good comfort, Master Ridley, and play the man. We shall this day light such a candle, by God's grace, in England, as I trust shall never be put out!"

By the heroic and lonely stand which he took, Micaiah takes rank with the kings and princes of the moral world. With Joseph, who said to the temptress, "How then can I do this great wickedness, and sin against God?" With Daniel, who opened his window toward Jerusalem and prayed to God, though he was cast into the lions' den for it. With John the Baptist, who rebuked Herod and Herodias for their sin. In the end, what looks like a lonely minority is always the majority. When Ahab was slain in the battle against which the prophet warned him and all Israel was scattered like sheep without a shepherd in the hill, where then were the four hundred false prophets?

There are students of our national life today who declare that the United States is in a moral decline, comparable to that which engulfed the Roman Empire. One of these observers said: "Everything is covered with dirt because the world has lost its morals." What we need above all else is a revival of Christian conscience, and of courage to testify to Christian standards in the court of a hostile world. When he was in the Tower of London, William Penn said, "My prison shall be my grave before I will budge a jot, for I owe my conscience to no mortal man." And John Bunyan in Bedford Jail, when offered release if he would promise to cease preaching, said, "Moss shall grow on these eyebrows before I surrender my principles or violate my conscience." It was that loyalty to conscience that qualified Bunyan to write that great tribute to conscience when he told of the passing of Mr. Honest:

When the day that he was to be gone was come, he addressed himself to go over the river. Now, the river at that time overflowed its banks in some places; but Mr. Honest in his lifetime had spoken to one Good-conscience to meet him there; the which also he did, and lent him his hand, and so helped him over.

NOTES

Mnason: An Old Disciple

Alexander Maclaren (1826–1910) was one of Great Britain's most famous preachers. While pastoring the Union Chapel, Manchester (1858–1903), he became known as "the prince of expository preachers." Rarely active in denominational or civic affairs, Maclaren invested his time in studying the Word in the original languages and in sharing its truths with others in sermons that are still models of effective expository preaching. He published a number of books of sermons and climaxed his ministry by publishing his monumental *Expositions of Holy Scripture*.

This message was taken from *Week-Day Evening Addresses*, published by Funk and Wagnalls in 1902.

ALEXANDER MACLAREN

2

Mnason: An Old Disciple

One Mnason of Cyprus, an old disciple, with whom we should lodge. (Acts 21:16)

THERE IS SOMETHING THAT stimulates the imagination in these mere shadows of men that we meet in the New Testament story. What a strange fate that is to be made immortal by a line in this book—immortal and yet so unknown! We do not hear another word about this host of Paul's, but his name will be familiar to men's ears until the world's end. This figure is drawn in the slightest possible outline with a couple of hasty strokes of the pencil. But if we take even these few bare words and look at them, feeling that there is a man like ourselves sketched in them, I think we can get a real picture out of them. Even this dim form crowded into the background of the apostolic story may have a word or two to say to us.

His name and his birthplace show that he belonged to the same class as Paul. That is, he was a Hellenist, or a Jew by descent, but born on Gentile soil and speaking Greek. He comes from Cyprus, the native island of Barnabas, who may have been a friend of his. He was an "old disciple," which does not mean simply that he was advanced in life but that he was "a disciple from the beginning," one of the original group of believers. If we interpret the word strictly, we must suppose him to have been one of the rapidly diminishing nucleus who thirty years or more ago had seen Christ in the flesh and had been drawn to Him by His own words. Evidently the mention of the early date of his conversion suggests that the number of his contemporaries was becoming few, and that there was a certain honor and distinction conceded by the second generation of the church to the survivors of the primitive band. Then, of course, as one of the earliest believers, he must, by this time, have been advanced in life.

A Cypriote by birth, he had emigrated to and resided in Jerusalem, and there must have had means and heart to exercise a liberal hospitality. Though a Hellenist, like Paul, he does not seem to have known the apostle before, for the most probable rendering of the context is that the disciples from Caesarea, who were traveling with the apostle from that place to Jerusalem, "brought us to Mnason," implying that this was their first introduction to each other. But though probably unacquainted with the great teacher of the Gentiles—whose ways were looked on with much doubt by many of the Jerusalem Christians—the old man, relic of the original disciples as he was, had full sympathy with Paul and opened his house and his heart to receive him. His adhesion to the apostle would no doubt carry weight with the "many thousands of Jews . . . which believe[d]; and they [were] all zealous of the law" (Acts 21:20), and were as honorable to him as helpful to Paul.

Now if we put all this together, does not the shadowy figure begin to become more substantial? And does it not preach to us some lessons that we may well take to heart?

Hold Fast to Early Faith

The first thing that this old disciple says to us out of the misty distance is—*Hold fast to your early faith, and to the Christ whom you have known.*

Many a year had passed since the days when perhaps the beauty of the Master's own character and the sweetness of His own words had drawn this man to Him. How much had come and gone since then—Calvary and the Resurrection, Olivet and the Pentecost. His own life and mind had changed from buoyant youth to sober old age. His whole feelings and outlook on the world were different. His old friends had mostly gone. James indeed was still there, and Peter and John remained until this present, but most had fallen on sleep. A new generation was rising round about him, and new thoughts and ways were at work. But one thing remained for him what it had been in the old days, and that was Christ. "One generation cometh and another goeth, but the Christ abideth for ever."

> We all are changed by still degrees;
> All but the basis of the soul.

And the "basis of the soul," in the truest sense, is that one God-laid foundation on which whosoever builds shall never be confounded nor ever need to change with changing time. Are we building there? And do we find that life, as it advances, tightens our hold on Jesus Christ, who is our hope.

There is no fairer nor happier experience than that of the old man who has around him the old loves, the old confidences, and some measure of the old joys. But who can secure that blessed unity in his life if he depends on the love and help of even the dearest or on the light of any creature for his sunshine? There is but one way of making all our days one, because one love, one hope, one joy, one aim binds them all together; and that is by taking the abiding Christ for ours and abiding in Him all our days. Holding fast by the early convictions does not mean stiffening in them. There is plenty of room for advancement in Christ.

No doubt Mnason, when he was first a disciple, knew but very little of the meaning and worth of his Master and His work compared with what he had learned in all these years. And our true progress consists not in growing away from Jesus but in growing up into Him. It consists not in passing through and leaving behind the first convictions of Him as Savior, but in having these verified by the experience of years, deepened and cleared, unfolded and ordered into a larger, though still incomplete, whole. We may make our whole lives helpful to that advancement. Blessed shall we be if the early faith is the faith that brightens until the end—and brightens the end. How beautiful it is to see a man, below whose feet time is crumbling away, holding firmly by the Lord whom he has loved and served all his days, and finding that the pillar of cloud, which guided him while he lived, begins to glow in its heart of fire as the shadows fall and is a pillar of light to guide him when he comes to die.

Dear friends, whether you be near the starting or near the prize of your Christian course, "cast not away therefore your confidence, which hath great recompense of reward" (Heb. 10:35). See to it that the knowledge of the Father, which is the little children's possession, passes through the strength of youth, and the "victory that overcometh the world" (1 John 5:4) into the calm knowledge of Him that is from the beginning, wherein the fathers find their earliest convictions deepened and perfected. "Grow in grace, and in the knowledge" (2 Peter 3:18) of Him whom to know ever so imperfectly is eternal life, whom to know a little better is the true progress for men, whom to know more and more fully is the growth and gladness and glory of the heavens. Look at this shadowy figure that looks out on us here and listen to His far off voice exhorting us all "that with purpose of heart [we should] cleave unto the Lord" (Acts 11:23).

Welcome New Thoughts and Ways

But there is another, and, as some might think, opposite lesson to be gathered from this outline sketch, namely, *the welcome that we should be ready to give to new thoughts and ways.* It is evidently meant that we should note Mnason's position in the church as significant in regard to his hospitable reception of the apostle. You can fancy how the little knot of "original disciples" would be apt to value themselves on their position, especially as time went on and their ranks were thinned. They would be tempted to suppose that they must understand the Master's meaning a great deal better than those who had never known Christ after the flesh. No doubt they would be inclined to share in the suspicion with which the thoroughgoing Jewish party in the church regarded this Paul, who had never seen the Lord. It would have been very natural for this good old man to have said, "I do not like these newfangled ways. There was nothing of this sort in my younger days. Is it not likely that we, who were at the beginning of the gospel, should understand the gospel and the church's work without this new man coming to set us right? I am too old to go in with these changes." All the more honorable is it that he should have been ready with an open house to shelter the great champion of the Gentile churches and, as we may reasonably believe, with an open heart to welcome his teaching. Depend on it, it was not every old disciple that would have done as much.

Now, does not this flexibility of mind and openness of nature to welcome new ways of work, when united with the persistent constancy in his old creed, make an admirable combination? It is one rare enough at any age, but especially in elderly men. We are always disposed to rend apart what ought never to be separated, the inflexible adherence to a fixed center of belief, and the freest ranging around the whole changing circumference. The man of strong convictions is apt to grip every trifle of practice and every unimportant bit of his creed with the same tenacity with which he holds its vital heart, and to mistake obstinacy for firmness and dogged self-will for faithfulness to truth. The man who welcomes new light, and reaches forward to greet new ways, is apt to delight in having much fluid that ought to be fixed, and to value himself on a "liberality" which simply means that he has no central truth and no rooted convictions. And as men get older they stiffen more and more, and have to leave the new work for new hands and the new thoughts for new brains. That is all in the order of nature, but so much the finer is it when we do see old Christian men who join to their firm grip of the old gospel the power of welcoming and, at least, bidding God speed, to new thoughts and new workers and new ways of work.

The union of these two characteristics should be consciously aimed at by us all. Hold unchanging, with a grasp that nothing can relax, by Christ our life and our all; but with that tenacity of mind, try to cultivate flexibility too. Love the old, but be ready to welcome the new. Do not consecrate your own or other people's habits of thought or forms of work with the same sanctity that belongs to the central truths of our salvation. Do not let the willingness to entertain new light lead you to tolerate any changes there. It is hard to blend the two virtues together, but they are meant to be complements, not opposites, to each other. The fluttering leaves and bending branches need a firm stem and deep roots. The firm stem looks noblest in its unmoved strength when it is contrasted with a cloud of light foliage dancing in the wind. Try to imitate the persistency and the open mind of that "old disciple" who was so ready to welcome and entertain the apostle of the Gentile churches.

Beauty in an Obscure Life

But there is still another lesson which, I think, this portrait may suggest, and that is, the *beauty that may dwell in an obscure life*. There is nothing to be said about this old man but that he was a disciple. He had done no great thing for his Lord. No teacher or preacher was he. No eloquence or genius was in him. No great heroic deed or piece of saintly endurance is to be recorded of him, but only this, that he had loved and followed Christ all his days. And is not that record enough? It is a blessed fate to live forever in the world's memory with only that one word attached to his name—a disciple.

The world may remember very little about us a year after we are gone. No thought, no deed may be connected with our names beyond some narrow circle of loving hearts. There may be no place for us in any record written with a person's pen. But what does that matter if our names, dear friends, are written in the Lamb's Book of Life with this for a sole epitaph: "a disciple"? That single phrase is the noblest summary of a life. A thinker? A hero? A great man? A millionaire? No, "a disciple." That says all. May it be your epitaph and mine!

What he could do he did. It was not his vocation to go into the regions beyond like Paul, to guide the church like James, to put his remembrances of his Master in a book like Matthew, or to die for Jesus like Stephen. But he could open his house for Paul and his company, and so take his share in their work. "He that receiveth a prophet in the name of a prophet shall receive a prophet's reward" (Matt. 10:41). He that with understanding and sympathy welcomes and sustains the prophet, shows thereby that he stands on the same spiritual level and has the makings of a prophet in him, though he lack the intellectual force and may never open his lips to speak the burden of the Lord. Therefore, he shall be one in reward as he is in spirit. The old law in Israel is the law for the warfare of Christ's soldiers. "As his part is that goeth down to the battle, so shall his part be that tarrieth by the stuff: they shall part alike" (1 Sam. 30:24). The men in the rear who guard the camp and keep the communications open may deserve honors, crosses, and prize-money as much as their comrades who led the charge that cut through the enemy's line and scattered their ranks. It does not matter what we do, so far as the real spiritual worth of the act is concerned, but only why we do it. All deeds are the same that are done from the same motive and with the same devotion. He who judges not by our outward actions, but by the springs from which they come, will bracket together as equals at last many who were widely separated here in the form of their service and the apparent magnitude of their work.

"She hath done what she could" (Mark 14:8). Her power determined the measure and the manner of her work. One precious thing she had, and only one, and she broke her one rich possession that she might pour the fragrant oil over His feet. Therefore, her useless deed of utter love and uncalculating self-sacrifice is crowned by praise from His lips, whose praise is our highest honor, and the world is still "filled with the odour of the ointment" (John 12:3).

So this old disciple's hospitality is strangely made immortal, and the record of it reminds us that the smallest service done for Jesus is remembered and treasured by Him. Men have spent their lives to win a line in the world's chronicles which are written on sand and have broken their hearts because they failed. This passing act of one obscure Christian, in sheltering a little company of travel-stained wayfarers, has made his name a possession forever. "Seekest thou great things for thyself? seek them not" (Jer. 45:5). But let us fill our little corners doing our unnoticed work for the love of our Lord, careless about man's remembrance or praise, because sure of Christ's, whose praise is the only fame, whose remembrance is the highest reward. "God is not unrighteous to forget your work and labour of love" (Heb. 6:10).

NOTES

Malchus: To Christ for Healing Love

Walter A. Maier (1893–1950) was known around the world as the speaker on "The Lutheran Hour," heard over more than a thousand radio stations. Many of his faithful listeners did not realize that this effective communicator was also professor of Old Testament and Semitic Languages at Concordia Seminary in St. Louis. It was said that Maier spent one hour in preparation for each minute that he spoke on the radio. Many of his radio sermons were published in volumes still treasured by those who appreciate good preaching.

This sermon was found in *Peace Through Christ*, published by Concordia Publishing House, St. Louis, in 1940.

WALTER A. MAIER

3

Malchus: To Christ for Healing Love

He touched his ear, and healed him. (Luke 22:51)

Blessed Jesus:

We come before Thee, our souls wounded by sin, to secure Thy healing benediction and Thy cleansing power. O Jesus, where can we find the cure for the selfishness and the sorrow that burden our lives, if not in Thee, our loving Savior, through a trusting approach to Thy cross? Let all else in life recede; but may the picture of the crucifixion which these Lenten weeks draw before our inner eye be irremovably etched on our hearts, so that we may always look to Thee for help! Send Thy healing mercy to our bruised spirits and broken lives! Show them, as Thou hast shown us, what an all-gracious Redeemer, ever faithful Friend of sinners Thou art to them that love Thee, our Christ and our God! Amen.

FOR MILLIONS IN THE United States eventually it must be either Christ and His redemption or chaos and its despair. More than a thousand people write us every day, and if you want to survey the reaches of sorrow, examine the towering files of our mail. Here are snatches from last week's letters sent by heartbroken, peace-robbed listeners. A theological student in Georgia, a young man who is to give others spiritual comfort, writes, "I have lost all hope and have been at the point of taking my own life." An eighty-one-year-old mother in Virginia confides, "I am writing to tell you how fearful I am that I may drop into hell because of my wickedness. I can see no hope of salvation. God does not answer me." A distracted wife in New Jersey fairly screams, "It is awful to live without hope. I have been tempted very often to take my own life."

What can we tell these stricken souls? What assurance can we give those battered and broken by a thousand crushing sorrows? What comfort, indeed, if not the hope offered in this Lenten appeal:

To Christ for healing love!

May God's Spirit richly bless this plea, based on Luke's inspired record: "He [Jesus] touched his ear and healed him."

Malchus Experienced That Healing Love

These words take us to the Garden of Gethsemane. Only a few days before this solemn Thursday, Jesus was welcomed to Jerusalem with enthusiastic acclaim. Now a mob, armed with swords and staves, has come to kill Him! Only a few hours earlier the Savior held His final meeting with the disciples in the Upper Room and at that Last Supper instituted Holy Communion, with the blessed gift of His own body and blood. Now the time has arrived when that body, scourged and wounded, will be given into death for our sins and that blood will flow from His beaten back, His nail-pierced hands and feet. Only a few moments before, in the deepest loneliness history knows, Jesus threw Himself to the ground, pleading in never-to-be-measured anguish that, if it were His Father's will, the cup of suffering might be lifted from His lips—so terrifying was the ordeal confronting Him, the Son of God, about to bear the world's sins in His own sinless body. Now the silence in the garden of prayer is suddenly broken.

From all sides, it seems, an armed mob thirsting for blood swarms into Gethsemane.

In this crisis it is a different Christ whom we behold in the revealing light of the full moon—no longer weak from that agonized wrestling, no longer terrorized into a blood-like sweat. With the courage imparted by the strengthening angel, He steps before that mob of murderers to ask, "Whom seek ye?" (John 18:4). When they answer, "Jesus of Nazareth" (v. 5), the Savior unhesitatingly identifies Himself with the words, "I am he" (v. 5). That declaration and the glance with which He pierced their hearts were so powerful that the whole throng was instantly hurled to the ground. The love of Christ was even stronger than His omnipotence. Though He could have avoided His arrest and the sequel of torture, uncomplaining Lamb of God that He is, He wanted to suffer for us!

He released the men who in a moment would take Him captive. After they had risen to their feet, their ranks seemed to part, and a sinister figure advanced toward Jesus. We recognize the form and features of that man whom all generations will despise because of his loathsome treachery—Judas, the disciple entrusted with the meager funds of the Twelve—Judas, the informer, the money-blinded wretch who, though repeatedly warned by Christ, sold his Savior and his own soul for thirty pieces of suicidal silver. His smirking kiss, it seems, fully aroused the disciples to their Lord's danger, and the hand of one of them nervously gripped the hilt of a sword hidden beneath his garment. Neither Matthew nor Mark nor Luke mentions the sword-bearing disciple's name. Only John identifies him as Peter. What an impressive example of Christian charity and forbearance in the silence of the first three evangelists! When their gospels were written, Peter was still alive, and with loving consideration they avoided mentioning his name to spare him and the early Christian congregation much sorrow. But John wrote toward the close of the first century, long after Peter had died, and, both for our warning and comfort, he could well record the name of this impetuous disciple.

How sorely we need that spirit of Christian charity today in helping to protect the good name of friend and foe! Newspapers employ and the public applauds peephole columnists who delight in publicizing private sins. We ourselves easily put the worst construction on the actions of others. Even nations can be goaded into warfare by propaganda later proved malicious falsehood. How the ministry suffers not only from front-page space devoted to its mistakes and from the motion-picture caricatures of the Protestant clergy as snooping hypocrites, but also through the unjustified attacks of scandal mongers and tongue waggers in some churches! We ask this audience to reject all unfounded attacks on the ministry. Instead, let us defend the clergy and by prayer and friendly help support these spiritual leaders, who, the most easily maligned of all men, have the hardest task the ministry ever faced in the United States.

In the heat of the excitement Peter, turning to Christ, asks, "Lord, shall we smite with the sword?" (Luke 22:49). Without waiting for an answer, he unsheathes his saber and with that single weapon tries to start a holy war. An ill-aimed blow strikes his nearest enemy—it happens to be the servant of the high priest—and cuts off his ear.

That was the beginning of bloodshed in the mistaken defense of Jesus Christ, but it was not the end. Recall the ill-fated attempt to tear Palestine from the Turks, as though some special holiness attached to the country that rejected Jesus! Think of the persecutions of the Waldensians and the Albigensians recorded in blood-dripping chapters! Someone has estimated that fifty million Protestants were massacred in persecutions and religious wars. This figure may be too high, but if the exact number were known, the total still would be appalling. We have had the sword-bearing, inquisitorial type of Christianity on this continent, too. In this age of many monuments we should recognize the first religious martyrs within the boundaries of what is now the United States and place a towering shaft at the mouth of Saint John's River in Florida. Sixty years before the Pilgrims landed at Plymouth Rock a French Protestant colony was established there.

But King Philip of Spain sent merciless Menendez to Florida to kill all the "Lutherans," as the French Protestants were known. Here and in nearby places during ensuing massacres at least five hundred men, women, and children, including the aged, the sick, the helpless, were cut down in cold blood, as the record specifically states, not because they were Frenchmen but because they were "Lutherans." The bloody horror was hardly over when those killers held religious services—"A cross was raised, and a site for a church selected on ground still smoking from the blood of a peaceful colony."

Why revive ancient history? Some of you may object. Why erect a monument in Florida to commemorate a carnage that everyone admits was a mistake? We answer: Because that obsession of spreading Christianity with the sword, far from being labeled an error, is often applauded. Last week a United States Federal Court indicted seventeen men on the charge of conspiring to overthrow the government of the United States. In their headquarters investigating agents found weapons, ammunition, and material for making bombs. Who were these men, organized, it is claimed, to overthrow our existing order by force of arms? Anarchists, radical agitators, atheistic Communists, agents of foreign nations? They called themselves the "Christian Front," employing Christ's holy name to justify a campaign of bloodshed. More significantly, they received encouragement from a publicized churchman. Instead of condemning their sword-bearing crusade, he declared, according to press reports, "I shall take my stand beside the Christian Fronters. I reaffirm every word I have ever said in support of their position."

What does Jesus say about such sword-bearing? Hardly had fire-breathing Peter severed that ear, when the Savior raised His voice in warning, "Put up again thy sword into his place: for all they that take the sword shall perish with the sword" (Matt. 26:52). That stern rebuke forever takes the sword out of any church's hand. It tells all Christian denominations to forget military power, political agitation, and lobbying for their special interests. It foretells that those who thus kill will themselves perish by violence. If only today this spirit of a militarized Christianity, this delusion of arms-bearing forces regimented to cut a bloody path for Christianity, were stopped in its tracks! How much more could be won by the love and the power of faith!

Jesus was not satisfied with rebuking His erring disciple. Even in the momentous hour of His own arrest and persecution He had a remedy for the wounded man and a lesson for Peter. There is plenty of negative preaching today with the repeated prohibitions, "Don't do this!" "Stop doing that!" Pulpit harangues and moralizing orations thunder accusations right and left. But Christ is the constructive Savior. He leaves no problem unsolved, no essential question unanswered. Here, too—and in less than twelve hours He will be nailed to the cross—He helpfully performs a miracle, the last in His earthly life. He stretches out the hand that never grasped the sword, touches the wounded ear, and His life-giving contact brings immediate healing.

The New Testament accounts tell us little about the man who had the distinction of being blessed by the Savior's last miracle. Three of the gospels do not even mention his name. The fourth simply calls him Malchus. What marvelous grace, however, that, though he was among Christ's enemies and a servant to those who lusted for our Lord's blood, the all-merciful Savior loved not only His friends but also those who opposed Him! How bitterly we, like Peter, hate! How quickly we fan our prejudices into consuming anger and resentment! Love our enemies? Some people cannot even love their own husband or wife or their own flesh and blood. Even if our soul's salvation were not involved in accepting Christ, we should follow Him, if only to learn how to love those who despise us and to do good to those who persecute us.

Malchus was a servant, a slave, of the high priest. When an acclaimed leader of men falls sick, every resource of healing is quickly drafted. Take the instance of Lord Tweedsmuir's critical illness. Outstanding specialists were rushed to his bedside;

carpenters quickly erected a special platform and approach at the depot; a private train was chartered to convey him to the best-equipped hospital in Canada; extraordinary traffic precautions were exercised throughout the trip. Everything humanly possible was done to help him, for Lord Tweedsmuir was a mighty man, the King of England's representative to the Canadian Dominion. But here, in our text, is a slave, a social outcast, one whose body and life are not even his own. And as though the Lord would tell all men, no matter how despised they may be, that He is their Savior, Jesus closes the long list of His pre-Calvary miracles by restoring the ear of a bondsman. Is not He, the condescending, all-loving Lord, the Redeemer whom you want? Is not His spirit the power we need to stifle the passionate hatreds that make people sneer at their fellowmen if their skin is of another hue, their families of another race, their worship of another creed?

Peter did not forget that rebuke and that miracle. Never again did he take recourse to the sword. After Pentecost and its outpouring of the Holy Spirit, the sword-wielding disciple became an apostle of patience. In his last days, when his enemies confronted him, as on that Maundy Thursday night they surrounded his Savior in the Garden, Peter did not start a second miniature holy war. Early records state that, when he was crucified for his loyalty, he asked that he be nailed to the cross head downward, since he did not regard himself worthy to die as his Lord had died. This is only tradition, but there can be no doubt that this humility agrees with Peter's spirit. Read his letters! He commits the punishment of evildoers to the government, not to the church. He says it is a thankworthy thing "if a man for conscience toward God endure grief, suffering wrongfully" (1 Peter 2:19). He holds up the example of the persecuted Christ, who, "when he was reviled, reviled not again; when he suffered, he threatened not" (v. 23). "Rejoice, inasmuch as ye are partakers of Christ's sufferings," he exults (4:13). Strengthened by the Spirit, fortified by faith's victories, he had learned to apply Christ's healing love.

We, Too, Can Find Healing in Christ

When we, too, know the healing power of Christ, we know the Savior aright. It was prophesied centuries before Gethsemane that the coming Deliverer of the race would be the Savior by "whose stripes [we are] healed" (2:24). The divine cure Jesus offers us today penetrates far deeper than physical pains and means much more than the healing of a lacerated ear or a wounded body. Christ, first of all, cures our souls of sin—that fatal illness for which men have no human help whatever, the inherited disease bequeathed to each of us at birth, and the contagion we contract during life. Only one cure can banish that soul-sickness—faith in the cleansing, life-transfusing blood of Jesus Christ. Only one contact can break the power of that soul- and body-destroying terror—the touch of Jesus Christ, our God and Savior. Only one prescription can present a permanent antidote for every form of this poison—the direction of the Master Physician's apostle: "Believe on the Lord Jesus Christ, and thou shalt be saved" (Acts 16:31). Only one hospital can offer a sure cure—the arms of Christ Himself and the restoring offered by the true church here on earth.

As we enter this Lenten season with its clinic for our inner life, let none of you spurn Christ's healing and claim self-confidently that you are of such spiritual health and moral perfection that you need no physician! Take inventory of your thoughts and impulses, your lusts and desires! Catalog the words that proceed from your lips—often hateful, malicious, dishonest, slanderous, untruthful! Recall each act that takes you away from God and perhaps brings injury or disgrace on yourself and others! See yourself as does God, whose eyes can penetrate your heart more completely than any X-rays, diagnosing your moral illness better than any corps of experts! And in honesty you must acknowledge yourself sick and sore, mortally afflicted by a poison inestimably more dangerous than the deadliest virus known to medical science.

Under the conviction of your sin listen to Christ as He repeats for you the first recorded sermon He ever preached,

"Repent ye, and believe the gospel" (Mark 1:15). Stand before the Crucified in true contrition—that is far more than mere sorrow over your sins, much deeper than good intentions to stop drinking, swearing, cheating, lying, slandering, coveting, serving fleshly lusts. Find real repentance which moves your soul with deep-rooted grief, unreserved confession of all your sins, known or unknown, and the realization that the breaking of God's Law is far more than a disobedience soon to be forgotten. As little as a cerebral hemorrhage can be stopped with a headache tablet, just so impossibly can the cure for sin be found without recognizing this divine decree: "The soul that sinneth, it shall die" (Ezek. 18:4, 20).

Thank God, "where sin abounded, grace did much more abound" (Rom. 5:20). In the darkness of any sin-blackened night you can see the rays of the cross pierce the gloom as, in fulfillment of the Old Testament promise, "the Sun of righteousness arise[s] with healing in his wings" (Mal. 4:2), that is, with the reviving powers radiated from Christ and His cross. When you train your eyes to behold Jesus nailed to that accursed timber, all else in life recedes. When your heart, crushed by sin and sorrow, acclaims the crucified Son of God your Savior, a greater power than that which healed Malchus's ear will cure your sin-sick soul forever. A score of diseases may baffle modern science, but Christ is stronger than any sin. Believe that, my young theological friend in Georgia distracted by the specter of suicide! Hundreds of thousands may die annually because they started treatment only when it was too late. But it is never too late for a penitent soul to come to Christ. Think of the promise of Paradise given to the malefactor on the cross, my eighty-one-year-old friend in Virginia! Vast multitudes in the United States are beyond the reach of proper medical care, but no one who believes the words I now proclaim across the country by the marvels of the radio, "The blood of Jesus Christ his Son cleanseth us from all sin" (1 John 1:7), has reason to cry out, "Oh that I knew where I might find Him!" (Job 23:3), for that sin-destroying Savior now stands in spirit before you to heal and help. Remember that, you in New Jersey who are continually tortured by the thoughts of self-destruction and attempted murder. Pay close attention, every one of you, particularly those whom God in His gracious guidance may have led especially to this broadcast for a holy purpose: Here is hope for your sin-sick souls! Here is help and strength from heaven itself, in this resolution of faith, "To Jesus Christ for healing love!"

Can Jesus also heal the sickness of the mind and the weaknesses of the body? Banish every doubt from your heart. The unlimited power of the blessed Savior, whose outstretched hand restored Malchus's ear in Gethsemane, can do today what He did in thousands of instances during His lifetime—when He drove out fevers, cured the palsy, healed the lepers, made the lame walk, restored sight to the blind, hearing to the deaf, and gave life to corpses. As definite proof of the healing power in Christian faith, we have specific instances, unnumbered in this audience alone, in which after medical science had exhausted its resources; after specialists had admitted, "As far as we can see, there is no hope"; after even the unmistakable signs of death had begun to show themselves, God suddenly exerted His quickening power. One of the leading surgeons here in Saint Louis, a physician who himself has performed thousands of major operations, expressly answered my question with this credo: "I believe that God Almighty can cure men and women today. I have repeatedly seen instances in which, after all human help had been tried without avail, the patient continued to live despite the prediction that he could not rally."

We will defend with all our energy this truth that Jesus can cure today as He did on that memorable night in the garden. But the decisive question is not, "Can Jesus heal?" but, "Will Jesus heal?" And here we must think in harmony with the revealed truth of the Scriptures. In the first-century church, we know, the apostles and others enjoyed a special gift of healing. They could lay their hands on diseased bodies and health would flow from that contact. Such cures were extraordinary endowments to the early church by which its power could be clearly manifested in those epochal days. But where in all the Scriptures is there a statement saying that today we must not bother about doctors? To the contrary, the Bible recognizes the necessity of physicians and of medicine, stating, "They that be whole need not a physician, but they that are sick" (Matt. 9:12).

So much fraud and deceit have been attached to the delusion that certain people, once they touch a disease-ridden body, can always bring miraculous healing, and so much sorrow has come from the similar error of trying to think ourselves out of our sicknesses that we must say a word in protest. From our files we take this account of an Altoona, Pennsylvania, "healing." In that city, on a recent May 13, a man who had been a bedfast invalid for seven months was carried to the platform of a "healer," anointed, and there, before the eyes of all, walked four or five steps. The tabernacle was in an uproar. The case was pronounced an outstanding cure. Twelve days later the man died from overexertion. His physician, a reputable doctor, declared, "It is my professional opinion that his trips to the tabernacle, the exertion, and the excitement . . . hastened his death." Here is the case of a twenty-eight-year-old Kansas City young man who, seriously injured, refused medical aid and preferred the help of a so-called "miracle woman." Because he was badly crushed, his strength kept ebbing away as he sat upright in his chair, praying for hours. After resisting twenty-four hours longer, he died. The family doctor, a registered physician, wrote, "Had that man received medical attention immediately, he would have had a good chance to get better." Thus have money-grabbing, falsehood, and despair often followed this misplaced trust.

Believe, however, that, if you pray to God for health or for the lifting of any other burden—the unpaid bills after the funeral of your deceased husband; the increasing mortgage charges of 1939, 1938, 1937, and longer, for which you see no source of payment; the sorrow in your family that seems beyond remedy—God can help you provided you are Christ's.

He will help you if this healing be according to His will. If our Lord prayed in that garden of agony, "Not my will, but thine, be done" (Luke 22:42), should we not go to dark Gethsemane and learn of Jesus to pray submissively for earthly blessings? God grants requests for the restoration of health, money, and happiness, for the removal of family friction and the lightening of all earthly burdens only when those petitions are in harmony with His good and gracious will, which—whether we understand it or not—always directs a Christian's life to a blessed end.

If you, my peace-robbed friends, tell me that though you are Christ's the Savior has not healed you, let me ask in reply whether you have that trusting, victorious faith which says, "Speak the word only, and my servant shall be healed!" (Matt. 8:8). Pray on your knees and with all your soul for a deeper, stronger, truer faith! Turn to the basic textbook on the curing of wounded hearts, the Bible! Daily, constantly, reverently, study the Word! Read it aloud! Have it explained to you! With this confident faith, all else may pass away, but the promise of God's healing grace positively must, through Christ, be fulfilled in your life. Perhaps, too, you have been dictatorial in asking for this healing love. You forget that sometimes God's will and wisdom must purify, refine, and strengthen your faith by repeated contact with the fires of adversity. Perhaps you have been too sure of yourself in the past, and therefore God sends no immediate help so that you may become truly humble, fully penitent, and completely reliant on Him. It may be that God has already helped you and you do not realize it because He has adopted a new and unexpected healing process.

Particularly do we ask you, our fellow-redeemed who have not found help for your sins and cure for your affliction in Jesus, to approach the cross and there to find your Savior and Substitute, your Ransom and Atonement. Keep His cross before your mind during the day and at night, when your eyes close or when they open in sleeplessness—cling to the Crucified! Then you will have not only a cure for every sin, a healing for every sorrow, but, day by day walking more closely with the crucified, now victoriously risen Savior, you can also look to the heavenly homeland with the confidence, "Earth hath no sorrow that heaven cannot heal!"

O Christ, grant every one of us Your healing love! Amen.

Caleb: An Old Testament Good Man

George W. Truett (1867–1944) was perhaps the best-known Southern Baptist preacher of his day. He pastored the First Baptist Church of Dallas, Texas, from 1897 until his death, and saw it grow in both size and in influence. Active in denominational ministry, Truett served as president of the Southern Baptist Convention and for five years was president of the Baptist World Alliance, but he was known primarily as a gifted preacher and evangelist. Nearly a dozen books of his sermons were published.

This sermon was taken from *We Would See Jesus,* published in 1915 by Fleming H. Revell.

GEORGE W. TRUETT

4

Caleb: An Old Testament Good Man

Caleb the son of Jephunneh. (Joshua 14:6)

OUR STUDY ONE SUNDAY MORNING was "Some Lessons from the Life of Barnabas." Barnabas was the Caleb of the New Testament, while Caleb was the Barnabas of the Old Testament. Not much is said in the Scriptures about Caleb, and yet enough is said to put him before us as one of the most inspiring examples of Old Testament history. He stands before us as a man of much dignity, of unbending devotion to principle, with a faith and a courage and a conviction after the very highest fashion. We do well to study the examples in the Bible of men who have wrought nobly in the cause of God. Such character study will point us lessons of how we may serve God to the best advantage.

Let us look, then, at some very meaningful lessons connected with this life story today. And, first, what of the character of Caleb? Barnabas, as we learned, was called "the son of consolation." Caleb may well be called the man of "all heart," and in the life story given of him in the Word of God there are certain manifestations that appear in the story that show how truly he might bear the name of Mr. Greatheart. See the out-flashing where his cheerfulness is one of the marked expressions of his life. You search in vain in this life story of Caleb to find a single instance where he was pessimistic or cheerless or dejected at all, but rather, the opposite shines out from his life story all along. He is one of the sunniest characters in all the Bible. Caleb had the New Testament spirit, enjoined long afterward by Paul, when Paul urged, "Rejoice evermore" (1 Thess. 5:16). And when again he said, "Rejoice in the Lord always: and again I say, Rejoice" (Phil. 4:4), Caleb had caught that spirit most graciously, and throughout his eventful life he was the man whose disposition was one of uniform and glorious cheerfulness. It is a most valuable lesson to learn, dear friends. "The joy of the Lord is jour strength." The dejected, moping, cheerless Christian, the one without joy, the one whose face indicates sorrow forever, is not the one who makes a gracious impression upon an unbelieving world. Caleb is a man, with all that hearty, cheerful, sunshiny life, to give men to understand how healthy and happy a thing it is for one to be a genuine Christian.

The manifestation of his heartiness of nature is also seen in the power he had to calm other people. You recall the report that the spies made when they came back from the land which they were sent to spy out for Moses. You recall the report they gave when they came back. Caleb and Joshua gave a gracious report. They did not minimize the difficulties at all. They said, "There are difficulties. The men are mighty. Their cities are well fenced. Their surroundings are such as to call for our earnest attention, but we are well able to overcome all the difficulties." That was their report. And then you remember the report of the other ten, their comrades. They gave an altogether different report. All the twelve agreed that it was a wonderful land, that it flowed with milk and honey, that the grapes of Eschol were not equaled by any other grapes, that everything about the land was inviting and glorious. But ten of them were overwhelmed with pessimism and unbelief. And when they had given their pessimistic report, all the people broke forth into wailing and whining, and dismay seized the whole congregation of Israel. And then Caleb stood up, this man of great heart, and calmed the whole crowd. He so spoke as to still them, at least for a season, in that time of dejection and gloom.

Here then is a vital lesson: The men who can tranquilize others are much needed men. They are of untold value to the world—the men who can tranquilize others. Almost any man can set other men by the ears. In a dozen sentences he can set men by the ears until they are ready to go at one another like untamed beasts. But the man who can tranquilize others, the man who can quell the spirit of the mob, the man who in state, in society, in the clashes that come with the classes, the man who can stand in their midst and still them, is a man of priceless value to any community. The man who can do that in a church, in the affairs of religion, the man who can quickly bring discordant and divided elements to fraternal and common standing ground for all, is a man of great price in the church of God. The one who can do that in the family, with the little frictions that come in the family life, who can suggest the way for the amicable adjustment of such little frictions, that one does a priceless work in family life. Now Caleb had that gracious power, the power of stilling others in the midst of tumultuous and unhappy experiences.

And, again, the manifestation of the greatheartedness of Caleb is seen in the fact that his whole life was filled with positive encouragement for other people. O my friends, the man who has the genius to encourage other people is the man this world is looking for and needs. The man who can put heart into men rather than take heart out of them, this world suffers and pants and languishes for such a man. Caleb had the noble genius for putting heart into men. There are men who have the evil genius of taking it all out. You can hear them for a dozen minutes and feel like you had been to a funeral or to something much worse. They can take the heart out of you. They can look at you in a way to make you feel a dozen years older. Caleb had the spirit of heartening men. He could send men out with a lofty, conquering spirit, and such a man is ever a man of invaluable moment in this world. When reverses come, when crops are bad, when business is dull, when collections go slowly, when health seems under its normal condition, the man who can step in then and put spirit and heart into the people, the man who has the genius to speak the word in season to them who are weary, he is a man that church, and state, and home, and society, and all classes and conditions most earnestly need. Caleb was that sort of a man.

And then he was a man to the last degree courageous in heart. When the ten gave their report, in which they dealt out the doleful story of the greatness of the giants in the land of Canaan, how large and mighty were their cities, what grasshoppers they felt themselves to be, the heart of all the people was ready to faint. Then Caleb stood in their midst and said, "Much that these ten men say is so. There are great men in the land we have visited, and their cities are large and mightily fortified, but we are well able to overcome them." Not only able, he said, but "well able" to overcome them. There is a man of the loftiest courage. Every one of us needs to cultivate the spirit of genuine and quenchless courage, for there is constant need of such courage in the daily battle of life that we must fight. There are so many reverses, surprises, and disappointments that come in the conflicts of human life, that every man needs, like Caleb, to cultivate the fortifying quality of courage. Oh, how weary the world is of whining, crying, pessimism, and discouragement! Every man needs to set himself, as did Caleb, to cultivating continually the noblest sort of courage for the battle of life.

See another striking element in Caleb's character. That was his conviction and fidelity to duty. Caleb was a man who dared to be in the minority. He was a man who could, without any blanching of face, go against the crowd. He was a man who had his anchorage thoroughly defined, and who adjusted himself in absolute obedience to the convictions his soul felt and knew to be right. He dared, therefore, to be in the minority. He dared, therefore, to go against the tumult of the crowd, in that he exhibited one of the most commendable elements, and one of the most forceful, that can be in a man's character. Alas, what sacrifices of truth, of principle, and of right are made because men do not dare to be in the minority!

In the world of politics, how men trim, and cavil, and cringe rather than go against the multitude. Caleb was a politician of the right sort, or rather, I should say, a statesman—a man who could be in the minority today because the minority was right, and who could patiently wait for tomorrow because ever is truth vindicated in due time. In society, in life's social relations, how many things are tolerated that people in their better natures rebel against. And yet they do not squarely brook the majority and say, "I will have no lot nor fellowship with this thing." One said to me recently, "I am ashamed every time I go through a certain social performance in this city." I replied, "Well, aren't you ashamed enough to turn the other way? Why yield pliantly to the spirit of the majority? Why not turn straight about, live honestly, be on good terms with your conscience, and squarely, with eagle eye, face the things that are wrong, and with courageous hands push them utterly aside?"

Caleb was a man who could stand out against the majority, looking to the revelation that the truth would have tomorrow and to the victory it would have. Oftentimes the majority are utterly wrong. That "the voice of the people is the voice of God" is oftentimes not so. Oftentimes the minority is right. And a man in the minority, with the consciousness that he is in alliance with truth and principle must be a man who, for no cause, would give up his convictions of right and truth and duty. Athanasius uttered the pronouncement, "I, Athanasius, against the world," and the stern theologian made the world hear and respect him.

Martin Luther went, against all the protestations of his friends, to the Diet at Worms, when they said, "It means your death." And Luther said, "I would go and declare what my soul knows to be right, if every tile on every roof in Wurtemberg were a devil." He won because he was true to principle. And Calvary, on which hung the Son of God, is the crowning expression of the truth that the minority is oftentimes the sublime winning force because it is right. Here, then, is an element in Caleb's character, priceless and powerful—his fidelity to duty against the majority.

Note again that Caleb was a man who was perennially young. That is one of the most beautiful things in his life story. Here was a man who never did get old. Now, at the advanced age of eighty-five years, he said, "I am as ready to go to war as I was forty-five years ago. I am just as strong for it, and I am as ready for it. I am as eager for the battle as I was back yonder at life's middle time." So there gleams out in the brief story of Caleb the delightful thought that he was a man who lived to the last breath of his life, young in spirit, and ever enthusiastic in his work. This is one of the most beautiful exhibitions of Caleb's remarkable character. You notice him at this advanced age of eighty-five years asking Joshua for the hardest job in all the kingdom. "Let me go up yonder and conquer Hebron, that city in the mountains, fortified so well and surrounded by the sons of Anak, those giants we heard about years ago. Let me have that hard task, and I will go and drive them out, even as Moses promised me forty-five years ago." And Joshua allowed him to go upon that difficult mission.

A man is already an old man who talks about "being let alone, having done his part." No man must talk like that in this brief and important life. A man's face must be set like a flint toward doing his duty until the last breath shall expire from his body. I say it today, from my heart of hearts, the very hour that I cannot heartily work for God, that hour I want to go home. There is not any place, there is not any need for any man ever to get old in this world. And if a man will link himself with the right things, and have the right viewpoint in the life he lives, he will never be an old man.

Moses was one hundred twenty years old when he died, but the Scriptures tell us that his eye had lost none of its brightness, nor was his natural force in any wise abated, and the reason is not hard to find. Moses had the right viewpoint for his life. Moses was linked with the right things. Moses had his anchorage first of all to God. He accepted the central truth of the Christian religion, that a man whom God has saved belongs utterly to God, to live or to die, to stay here or to go hence, according to God's will. Nor was that all in Moses' case. Moses linked himself with great causes for the lifting up of his oppressed fellows. Moses lived not a day for himself. Why should he? Moses was not concerned about his own ease or aggrandizement. Why should he be? Life is missed in its sublime meaning if any man lives for himself. Moses gave himself as a servant, with his marvelous powers of brain and heart; a servant to lift up poor, beaten, oppressed Israel. And Moses in self-forgetting sacrifice laid his life on the altar for the restoration of Israel to her proper place among the nations of the earth. No wonder he was still a young man when he died. You take men who live like that, and they are not old men.

Glorious spectacle was that of Gladstone, beyond eighty, with an eye yet bright, and with a mind well poised and keen and clear. Gladstone was linked with everything in the world that would make for the uplifting of humanity. And a man who thus links his life is not a man ever to get old. Caleb was perennially young, and at the advanced age of eighty-five Caleb asked for the hardest job that was ever given him in his life. "Let me have Hebron," he said. Hebron meant difficulty. Hebron meant battle. Hebron meant most exacting work. Hebron meant awful conflict. Hebron meant a fight to the finish. But there, at the advanced age of eighty-five, he said, "Put on my shoulders the hardest thing I have ever had to do, and I will go forth to the battle." And forth he went and won, to the everlasting credit of his name.

Oh, how stimulating that record is! Do you wish to make the most of life? Then do not seek the soft, easy places of life. Why should it matter to me if there should come home to me today the conviction that God would have me commit myself to dark and besotted Africa, to give myself in unstinted devotion to lifting up that race? Why should I halt a moment? I am not mine own, nor is a single power I possess mine own. I am

God's. Why should I not adjust myself to what He asks, I in my sphere, and you in yours? If you would make life truly great, great in its deepest and highest sense, get the viewpoint Caleb had. Do not look for the easy and soft places in life, but look for the places where you can have full opportunity to put every power of your nature on the altar for God, in the high service of humanity. Here is where many Christians fail. I haven't a question that many preachers largely fail because they are looking for easy and soft places. The one thing we are to think about, to care for, is that we may stand in the battle's front and in the thick of the fight, every man where God wants him, whether lawyer, doctor, minister, teacher, banker, farmer, or what not. If God has hard tasks, big jobs, and gigantic undertakings, let each one give himself to them with the spirit of Caleb, scorning easy places, asking for God to give him anything He wishes in His infinite wisdom and love.

I speak to men here today, a large company, and very few of them with gray hairs, but we will have them after a little if we live. Let us address ourselves to life's problems as did Caleb. Let us make up our minds never to get old, never. Let us make up our minds that we will never admit for a breath to ourselves that suggestion of the Devil that we have "done our part." Done our part! Done our part in life! Why, if we should live ten million years, and give every moment to the service of God, every drop of our blood, every thought of our brain, we would then have barely made a start in giving to God that which He so rightfully deserves at our hands. Let Caleb teach us. Let him teach us how always to be young.

I know some old men, and you do, too, as the world counts it, that are not old at all. They are as young as lads of twenty-one. They are linked with great causes. They are forgetting themselves. They hear the heartbeat of a suffering world. They plan, they give, they love, they go, and they serve, forgetting self. They will never get old, but like Caleb they will come down to the end at last with perennial youth.

But see again Caleb's case. Caleb "wholly followed the Lord

his God" (see Num. 32:12; Deut. 1:36; Josh. 14:8–9, 14). That is what the Scripture says again and again about him. And that is the secret, the sublime secret, of all the other wonderful elements of his character we have been considering. Caleb wholly followed the Lord his God. Whenever a man does that, what does he care for the clamor of the multitudes? Whenever a man does that, what does he care for the view of the majority? Whenever a man does that, what does he care for anything except the "well done" of the God whom he serves? Caleb wholly followed the Lord his God. Caleb said that for himself, "I have wholly followed Him." And Moses said it about Caleb. And God Himself said, "My servant, Caleb, has wholly followed Me." So that he had the testimony overwhelming of the reality of his devotion to God.

Now in that fact resides the sublime secret of Caleb's marvelous power for God. And just there is the pivotal point upon which is determined man's relation to God and His relation to man. Here is where men are undone. If men do not follow God definitely and wholeheartedly, if men do not follow God, putting the reins of their lives into His hands, then such men make practical shipwrecks of Christian usefulness and Christian joy. The supreme peril to us all is that we take our religion too easily. Our religion is not some nice bandbox affair. Our religion means battle and suffering and service. Our religion means the forgetting of self. Our religion is to soothe the brow of every aching head, to give glad cheer to every cheerless heart, and to lift up every fallen life. The constant trouble is that we take our religion too easily.

Caleb's spirit is the spirit for us all—wholehearted devotion to God. Oh, for that spirit, which found its expression in Paul, which found its expression in Luther, which found its expression in Wesley, which found its expression in Knox, which found its expression in Spurgeon, which found its expression in David Brainerd. Brainerd said, "I had rather win one poor lost soul for Christ than to win mountains of gold and silver for myself." That is the spirit that will consume the evil of the world and take away its chaff and make life a great and sublime thing. That is the spirit Caleb had, and that is the spirit for us all.

I do not wonder that many Christians get so little out of religion. The explanation is at hand. They put so little into it. I do not wonder that most of the time they stumble along in the dark. They live in the dark. I do not wonder that all along they are swept with conflicting emotions. They put themselves where such emotions can have the fullest sway. The Christian life is not to be lived in the twilight. The Christian life is to be open, aboveboard, straightforward, definite, and pronounced. The man who lives that sort of a Christian life reaches up any time with his hand and touches the hand of Christ. Caleb lived that sort of a life. O friends, if you would have power in your family, where some are gainsaying and ungodly, if you would have power in life's social relations or business relations, as you touch elbows with men, then yield never one iota to the admission of the wrong thing into your life. Stand like Caleb, with wholehearted devotion to God.

Just here, I say, is the explanation for a thousand ills in human life. I talked yesterday at length with a strong businessman upon whom troubles have recently come with terrible force and fury. Years ago, when I preached in another place, he found Christ and nobly confessed Him. Now he is down in the dark and deep valley of distress. He said, "I have come a long distance to go over this matter with you." I said, "The physician must diagnose his case before he is willing to give any medicine. Now, answer me, first, some questions honestly, and we will go over the whole matter." And when I probed the man with questions, I could not find that he had one religious habit in his life which he lived up to with a day's consistency—not one. He said, "Why, I see after my business on Sunday. I have not read my Bible for months. I go to church with awful irregularity, and I can hardly tell you when I did go alone and get down and utter a prayer." I said, "You have come this distance to ask me to tell you the trouble. You do not need that I tell you that you have trifled with your profession, and are trifling with your Savior, and are trifling with your church, and are trifling with the Scripture, and are trifling with everything holy. You want to know why you have doubts? You have only to use your mind a second to find out. You want to know why you have no peace and no joy? You want to know why the joy of those other years is all gone—that zest, that interest in religion? The answer is right at your side. There is no conscientious devotion in your life to God, nor will you have those bright, blessed days again until you play the man for the Almighty."

Oh, my friends, God is my witness, there never passes a day that the most fervent prayer of my soul for you is not offered that you may wholly follow God! Oh, I grieve beyond what you can know, to see you living any double, halfhearted life. I grieve to see you missing that steadfast joy and that Christian power that can only come to the men who walk as Caleb walked, who are straightforward and pronounced, and who give the benefit of the doubt always to God and never to themselves. It comes to me again and again what a brother said some time ago in this church, that for a long while he just had enough religion to make himself thoroughly miserable, to give him a kind of a toothache feeling. You know exactly what he meant. He was living a halfhearted life. There is the explanation of ten thousand troubles in the Christian life. Men do not wholly follow God. Let Caleb teach us at that vital point, for here is the real secret of his masterful life.

The hour is past. You will indulge me this other word. What was the result of it all in Caleb's life? God gave him long life. Nor was that all. God gave him continued opportunity and strength to serve Him with that long life, so that in his old age, at eighty-five, he had the greatest victory that he had ever had in all his life. Oh isn't it glorious for a person to grow old like that? The other day an old preacher came into one of our Workers' Conferences, and he said, "I preached yesterday to my people, and my text was, 'That I might finish my course with joy!" He said, "I was hedging for myself. I want to finish my course with joy, not to finish it soured and embittered and pessimistic, making everybody miserable about me, but I mean, by God's grace, to finish my course with joy." He said, "I told my country church yesterday I was going in to serve them with more zeal and love than ever before." He will not get old. He will not be a misery to his children and grandchildren. He has the right viewpoint of life. Caleb had it, and God gave him increased opportunity and strength as a great leader, and then God rewarded him with the great possession that forty-five years before he had seen. And then, with it all, God gave him rest.

O soul, is Caleb's God yours? Receive Him today to be yours and follow that God like Caleb followed Him. And if you are here today with all sorts of subterfuges and evasions and speculations and doubtful questions in your life, just be done with them, and just be straightforward and pronounced and true, like Caleb, to God. And your light and day and usefulness in the Christian life will grow brighter and brighter, even until that blissful day when you shall hear the Master say, "It is enough; come home, My friend, to be forever with the Lord."

NOTES

Jeroboam's Wife: A Hearer in Disguise

Charles Haddon Spurgeon (1834–1892) is undoubtedly the most famous minister of the nineteenth century. Converted in 1850, he united with the Baptists and soon began to preach in various places. He became pastor of the Baptist church in Waterbeach, England, in 1851, and three years later he was called to the decaying Park Street Church, London. Within a short time, the work began to prosper, a new church was built and dedicated in 1861, and Spurgeon became London's most popular preacher. In 1855, he began to publish his sermons weekly; today they make up the fifty-seven volumes of *The Metropolitan Tabernacle Pulpit*. He founded a pastor's college and several orphanages.

This sermon was taken from *The Metropolitan Tabernacle Pulpit,* volume 10.

CHARLES HADDON SPURGEON

5

Jeroboam's Wife: A Hearer in Disguise

And it was so, when Ahijah heard the sound of her feet, as she came in at the door, that he said, Come in, thou wife of Jeroboam; why feignest thou thyself to be another? for I am sent to thee with heavy tidings. (1 Kings 14:6)

AHIJAH THE PROPHET WAS blind. Did I not tell you this morning that God's servants could be happy without the light of the sun? If God should be pleased to deprive their natural eyes of the pleasures of light, their souls would not be without joy, for as in the New Jerusalem so in the renewed heart: "The glory of God did lighten it, and the Lamb is the light thereof" (Rev. 21:23). Doubtless this was the case with that venerable prophet. He was not like Moses, whose eye did not wax dim and whose natural strength did not abate, but his eyes were set with age. The organs of vision had so decayed through the multitude of his years that he could not see so much as a ray of light. Yet doubtless when he could not look out of the windows, God looked in. When there was no beam coming in from the sun, much light was darted in from heaven.

What man of modern times saw more than blind Milton? It would be well for us to feel the influence of that "drop serene," and close our eyes forever, if we could but see such visions of

God as Milton has penned in his *Paradise Lost* and *Paradise Regained.* Here is a fine picture for you. Behold the venerable prophet sitting alone in his humble cottage, and yet not alone because his God is with him. Blind, but yet in the highest sense a seer, looking into the invisible and by faith beholding things that we blind men who have our sight can never see. Beholding what eye has not seen, and hearing what ear has never heard.

This then may furnish a word of comfort at the outset to any who are suffering some infirmity: Jesus can recompense you. You are not the only persons who have been called so to suffer. Full many of your humble guild—the company of the blind—have been gifted with spiritual sight. If you have lost hearing or the use of any of the members of your body, remember that no strange thing has happened to you but such as is common to man. There is a way by which, in proportion as your tribulations abound, so your consolations may abound through Jesus Christ. No, these very privations that you feel so sadly, that so loudly demand our sympathy, may by God's love be transmuted into mercies by a holy alchemy, which really turns iron into gold. He can turn your losses into gains, and your curses into blessings.

Mark well this venerable prophet—a man so old as to have survived the senses that give life its charm—is it not time for him to die? Has he not outlived his usefulness when he is made entirely dependent upon his fellow creatures and a burden to himself? Why does not the prophet's Master send a convoy of angels to take the good man home? There he sits without any apparent perception of the scenes transpiring around him. Surely, surely it is time for the Master to call him away! But no, He does not. Ahijah must not die. He has another message to deliver, and he is immortal until his work is done. I have no doubt he sweetly slept after he had delivered his last message, but not until then. Brothers and sisters, you and I have no right to want to go to heaven until our work is done. There is a desire to be with Christ which is not only natural but spiritual. There is a sighing to behold His face, which if a man be without I shall question if he be a Christian at all. But to wish to be away from the battle before we win the victory and to desire to leave the field before the day is over is nothing but laziness and listlessness. Therefore, let us pray to God to save us from it.

Whitfield and a company of ministers were talking together and expressing their desire to go to heaven. Good Mr. Tennant was the only man who differed from them. He said he did not wish to die. He thought that if his brother Whitfield would but consider for a time he would not wish to be gone either. He said, "If you hire a man to do a day's work, and he is saying all the day, 'I wish it were evening' or 'I wish it were time to go home,' you would think, 'What a lazy fellow he is.' You would wish you had never engaged him. So," he said, "I am afraid, it is nothing but our idleness that often prompts us to desire to be away from our work." If there be a soul to win, let me not stop until I have won it. Truly some of us might summon up courage enough to say, "I would fain barter heaven for the glory of Christ, and not only wait twenty years out of heaven if I may have twenty years of glorifying Him the better, but wait out altogether if I may outside heaven sing to Him sweeter songs and honor Him more than I can inside its walls. Outside heaven shall be heaven to me if it shall help me to glorify my Lord and Master the better."

You have heard, I dare say, that anecdote of good Mr. Whitfield in his early ministry lying down, as he thought, to die in a high fever, and a poor woman sitting by his side and tending him. In his sad moments Whitfield thought of dying, but the woman said, "No, master Whitfield, you are not to die yet. There are thousands of souls to bring to Christ, so keep up your spirits for you must live and not die—your Master has yet work for you to do." All this comes to my mind as I think of that venerable old prophet sitting in his chair waiting until he shall have spoken to Jeroboam's wife, and then after that ascending to his Father and his God—but not until his work was done.

We have introduced to you Ahijah, the venerable prophet. We must now address an incident connected with his closing ministry. In the text, we have before us *an occasional hearer.* Secondly, we observe a *useless disguise.* Thirdly, we *listen to heavy tidings.*

The Occasional Hearer

We have before us, first of all, the occasional hearer. Jeroboam and his wife did not often go to hear Ahijah. They were not people who went to worship Jehovah. They neither feared God nor regarded his prophet. There may be some such here tonight. You do not often come to a place of worship. I am glad you are here now. It may be my Master has sent me with tidings for you. Give earnest heed that the tidings may be received and blessed. I am sometimes tired of preaching to those who hear me every Sunday, for I fear some of them never will be saved. They get hardened by the gospel, all the blows of the hammer have only tended to weld their hearts to their sins and make them harder instead of melting them. May God grant, however, that my fears may be removed and that some who have long resisted the wooings of the gospel may yet yield. I have more hope of you occasional hearers. I know that when my Master has helped me to cast the net on the right side of the ship I have taken some of you. There are among those numbered with us some of the best in the church, and the most useful men in our society, who were brought in by dropping into the place just as stray hearers—passing by, perhaps, or coming out of curiosity. But God knew who they were. He knew how to adapt the sermon to the case and affect the heart with the Word.

Now, here was an occasional hearer, and we make the observation that *this occasional hearer was totally destitute of all true piety.* Most occasional hearers are. Those who have true religion are not occasional hearers. You will find that truly gracious persons are diligent in the use of the means. Instead of thinking it a toil to come up to the place of worship, I know there are some of you who wish there were two Sundays in the week. The happiest times you ever have are when you are sitting in these seats and joining in our sacred songs.

> Thine earthly Sabbaths, Lord, we love.

There is no verse that gives you a better idea of heaven as a place than that—

> Where congregations ne'er break up,
> And Sabbaths have no end.

Gracious souls love the place where God's honor dwells, and the assembling of themselves together is always a blessed thing to them. But occasional hearers are generally graceless persons. I know how you spend your Sunday. There is the morning. You are not up very early. It takes a long time to dress on a Sunday morning. Then follows the Sunday paper with the news of the week, which must be gone through. The wife has been toiling hard all the morning with the dinner. What do you care? Then there is the afternoon when there is a little more lolling about. Then in the evening there is the walk. But the day, after all, is not very happy and comfortable. Sometimes you have wished there were no Sundays except that they give your body a little rest. You do not fear God, nor do you care for His service. Nevertheless, I am glad you have come. Who can tell? My Lord, who found out Jeroboam's wife, can find you out. Though it has been many days since you darkened the walls of God's sanctuary, this shall be the beginning of many such days to you. Who can tell? This may be your new-birth night. This may be when you shall turn over a new leaf. No, not turn over a new leaf, but get a new book altogether, and find your name written in the Lamb's Book of Life.

The second remark about these occasional hearers is, that when they do come, *they very generally come because they are in trouble.* When Jeroboam's wife came and spoke to the prophet, it was because the dear child was ill at home. I know some occasional hearers who go to a place of worship as people go to a chemist's shop—that is, when they want something because they do not feel quite right. Yes, your child is very sick. You have been watching all day, and you have thought, "I cannot stand it any longer. I will just walk out and go to a place of worship tonight. I want something to cheer me." You have had such trials lately that your wife said to you, "John, we must not keep on in this way any longer. It is clear all we do ends without any prosperity. We put our money into a bag that is full of holes. We spend it for that which is not bread. We labor for that which does not profit." So you have come here to see if the Lord may have a word of comfort through his servant who speaks to you. I can only say you are very welcome to come in, wife of Jeroboam. We are as glad to see you as though you always come, and we do hope that this sorrowful affliction may be overruled by God for your lasting good.

There are persons who profess to be atheists, but their atheism is not very deep. Addison tells us of a man who on board ship in a storm knelt down to pray and expressed his firm belief in a God. When he got ashore someone laughed at him for it, and he challenged the man to a duel. They fought together and the atheist fell wounded. When the blood was flowing he believed there was a God, and he began to cry to God with all his might to save him. The physician bound up the wound. The man put the question to him: "Is it mortal?" "No," he said, "it is only a flesh wound." Then, said the man, "There is no God; I am a thorough atheist." He believed in God when he thought he was going to die. The moment he felt himself better he returned to his unbelief. A pretty religion that to live in, and a pretty religion to die with!

Your absence from God's house will do very well when things go well with you. You can go out with a young wife to dissipate in frivolity hours that should be sacred to worship. But when sickness shall come, when affliction shall fall heavily upon you, when you have trial after trial and you yourself begin to get gray with many cares, and feeble and helpless with many years, and death comes near and casts his pale shadow across your cheek, and strange thoughts that are oblivious of all around come over you by day, and singular dreams that throw you into the company of the long since dead surprise you by night, and fears and frights and signs and calls and bodings of imagination prove the wanderings and weakness of your brain, then, but possibly not until then, you think of going to the house of God. I am glad, therefore, if this trouble has visited you early, or ever "the grinders cease because they are few, and those that look out of the windows be darkened"; and I am very glad that you have come to the house of God. Come in, wife of Jeroboam, for I bear you tidings from the God of heaven tonight.

There is a third point: *This woman would not have come but that her husband sent her on the grounds that he had heard Ahijah preach before.* It was this prophet who took Jeroboam's mantle and rent it in pieces, and told him he was to be king over the ten tribes. That message proved true. Therefore Jeroboam had confidence in Ahijah. There are some of you who at times used to hear the gospel. You have not been of late. But there were seasons when you did come up to God's house, and times when you used to tremble under God's Word. If I am not mistaken, there are men and women here tonight who once were conscience-stricken. The Word of God used to come home to you with exceeding great power and make you tremble. Did you not even profess faith in Christ? Why some of you were very busy at revival meetings, trying to bring others to the Savior. But your religion was like smoke out of the chimney. It has all blown away. Like early mist it was soon scattered when the sun had risen. Yet the remembrance of these things sticks by you now. You cannot help it. You feel there must be something in religion. The old stings that were in your conscience have not been quite extracted. Therefore, at the present moment, you are quite willing to listen to the

Word. Perhaps you are even hoping that it may come with true power now and save you after all. I wish I could wake the echoes of the slumbering consciences of some of you! O that I could recall the days of your youth, the times of your boyhood and girlhood, when you went up to the assembly of the saints to keep holy day. Those things you cannot quite forget. I pray that such remembrances may often turn your feet toward the place of worship.

We have brought out three points of character. They were persons of no piety. In trouble they sought the prophet. They had confidence in him because they had heard him preach before. But there is one more point: *They had one godly member of their family and that brought them to see the prophet.* Their child was sick and ill, and it was that which led them to inquire at the hands of the Lord. I hope there is no family here which has the misfortune to be without a believer in it. You, man, have no fear of God. But strange to say, the Lord has taken one out of your family to be a witness for Him. That daughter of yours, you sometimes jeer at her, but you know you value her. You used to send her to Sunday school just to get rid of her, but the Lord met with her. What a comfort she has been to you! How glad she has made your heart though you do not tell her so!

Perhaps the godly one in the family is like this young Abijah in the text. He is sick and near to die. You can recollect, though you do not fear God, how the darling boy was sick! How you sat by his little bed and took his hand in yours when it was scarcely anything but skin and bone! How he prayed for you at night that God would save father and mother and take them to heaven! How, just as he died, he looked on you with those bright eyes so soon to be filmed in death and said, "Father, will you not follow me?" Since that time you have often felt that something is beckoning you up yonder. Though you have gone on forsaking God and despising holy things, yet still there is a little link between you and heaven that is not snapped yet, and you sometimes feel it tugging at your heart. I pray God it may tug so hard tonight that your heart may go up to God and lay hold of Jesus the Savior of sinners.

What joy it causes me to think that God does call one out of a godless household because where there is one there is sure to be another before long. It is like putting a light into the midst of stubble, there will soon be a blaze. I have hope of a family when one child is converted, for grace is like precious ointment, it spreads a perfume all around. When a box of fragrant spice is put into a room, the perfume soon fills the entire chamber. It then creeps silently up the stairs into the upper rooms and ceases not its work until it has filled the whole house. So when there is true grace in a house, the Holy Spirit blesses its hallowed power until even the lodgers and family acquaintances begin to feel the influence of it. Is it your one praying child that has brought you here tonight? May God grant that he may be the means of bringing you to heaven as well.

But there is one sad reflection that should alarm the occasional hearer. Though Jeroboam's wife did come to the prophet that once and heard tidings, yet *she and her husband perished after all.* Oh! if there were a register kept of the many thousands who come inside the tabernacle gates and listen to our voice, I am afraid—I am sadly afraid—it would be found that there were many who did hear the tidings, and did tremble at them, too, who nevertheless contemned the counsels of the Most High, turned not at His rebuke, went on in their sin, and perished without hope. Shall it be so with any of you? Are you to be worms in hell? Will you make your bed among the flames? My hearers, will you die without God and without hope? Will you leap into the black unknown with no bright promise of the Savior to cheer you in the thick darkness? May God prevent it! May He be pleased to bring you to Christ, the rock of your salvation, that you may depend upon Him with your whole heart.

While thus speaking about the occasional hearer, an idea haunts my mind that I have been drawing somebody's portrait. I think there are some here who have had their character and conduct sketched out quite accurately enough for them to know who is meant. Do remember that if the description fits you, it is meant for you. If you yourself have been described, do not look about among your neighbors and say, "I think this is like somebody else." If it is like you, take it home to yourself, and God send it into the center of your conscience, so that you cannot get rid of it.

The Useless Disguise

Jeroboam's wife thought to herself, "If I go to see Ahijah, as he knows me to be the wife of Jeroboam, he is sure to speak angrily and give me very bad news." Strange to tell, though the poor old gentleman was blind, she thought it necessary to put on a disguise. So she doffed her best garment and put on a country woman's russet gown and away she went. She left the scepter and crown behind and took a basket, as though she had just come from market. In this basket she did not put gold, jewels, and silver, but a present such as a farmer's wife might bring. There were loaves, cracknels, and a cruse of honey. And as she went along, she thought, "The old gentleman will not know me." She traveled through her own dominions and nobody knew her. She went into the neighboring dominions of Judah as far as Shiloh, and she pleased her imagination with the thought, "How I shall deceive him. I will ask him a question, as if I were a plowman's wife. He will not know who I am. He will be pleased with my present and prophecy soft things concerning my child." How great was her surprise! No sooner did the blind prophet hear her footsteps than he said, "Come in, thou wife of Jeroboam; why feignest thou thyself to be another? for I am sent to thee with heavy tidings?" How she started back with astonishment! She had deceived hundreds who were blessed with eyes. But here was a man who could not be deceived, but found her out before she had opened her lips. He recognized her before she had time to test her sorry artifice or tell her subtle tale—"Come in, thou wife of Jeroboam."

I do not suppose there is anybody disguised here tonight, though such things may happen. The working man, who is afraid he shall be laughed at if he be known, may come here in disguise. Now and then a clergyman may come in who would not be very comfortable in his conscience if it were known he did such a thing, and so he does not show himself exactly in his wonted garb. Notwithstanding whoever you may be, disguised or not, it is of no use where God's gospel is preached. It is a quick discerner, and it will find out the thoughts and intents of the heart. It will search you out and unmask your true character, disguise yourself as you may.

Many come to God's house not disguised in dress, but still disguised in manner and appearance. How good you all look! When we sing and you take your books, how heavenly-minded you look! And when we pray, how reverent you are! How your heads are all bowed and your eyes covered with your hands! I do not know what you all say in your hats when you come in, and I should not like to know. I do not know how much praying there is when you sit in a devout posture, though you assume the attitude and compose your countenance as those who draw near to supplicate the Lord. I am afraid there are many of you who do not pray a word or present a petition, though you assume the posture of suppliants. When the singing is going on there are many who never sing a word with the spirit and the understanding. In the house of God I am afraid there are many who wear a mask, stand as God's people stand, sit as they sit, pray as they pray, and sing as they sing. But all the while what are you doing? Some of you have been attending to your children while we have been singing tonight. Some of you have been casting up your ledger, attending to your farms, scheming about your carpentering and bricklaying. Yet all the while if we had looked into your faces we might have thought you were reverently worshiping God. Oh! those solemn faces and those reverent looks, they do not deceive the Most High God. He knows who and what you are. As you are in His house, He sees you as clearly as men see through glass. As for hiding from the Almighty, how can you hide yourself from Him? You might as well attempt to hide in a glass case, for all the world is a glass case before God. When you look into a glass beehive, you can see the bees and everything they do. Such is this world, a sort of glass beehive in which God can see everything. The eyes of God are on you continually; no veil of hypocrisy can screen you from Him.

There may be some among you who occasionally sit here, some members of this church who after all may feign to be other than they are. It is a melancholy and a most solemn reflection that there are many who profess to be Christians who are not Christians. There was a Judas among the twelve. There was a Demas among the early disciples. We must always expect to find chaff on God's floor mingled with the wheat. I have tried, the Lord knows, to preach as plainly and as much home to the mark as I could, to sift and try you. But for all that the hypocrite will come in. After the most searching ministry, there are still some who will wrap themselves about with a mantle of deception. Though we cry aloud and spare not, and bid you lay hold on eternal life, yet, alas! how many are content with a mere name to live and are dead. Many come here and even hold office in the church. Yes, the minister himself may even preach the Word and after all be hollow and empty. How many who dress and look fair outside are as John Bunyan said, only fit to be tinder for the Devil's tinderbox, for they are all dry and sere within! God save as from a profession if it be not real. I pray that we may know the worst of our case. If I must be damned, I would sooner go to hell unholy than as a hypocrite. That back door to the pit is the thing I dread most of all. Oh! to sit at the Lord's table and to drink of the cup of devils! To be recognized among God's own here, and then to find one's own name left out when He reads the muster-roll of His servants, oh, what a portion for eternity.

I bid you tear off this mask, and if the grace of God is not in you, I pray you go into the world where will be your fitting place and abstain from joining the church if you are not really a member of the body of Christ. You see why I urge this. Because no dressing up, however neatly it may be done, can conceal us from God. Oh! how some who have been fair on earth have been startled when they thought they were going into heaven! They had their foot almost on the doorstep, but the angel came and said, "Get gone, wife of Jeroboam. I know whom you are. You could deceive the minister. You could deceive the deacons. You could get baptized and join the church. But you cannot enter here. Get gone. Your portion is with the filthy in the pit of hell." O, may He never say this to you and me. But may we all be so real here that He may say, "Come, ye blessed of my Father, inherit the kingdom prepared for you from the foundation of the world" (Matt. 25:34). "Thou God seest me!" (Gen. 16:13). Write that on the palm of your hand and look at it. Wake up in the morning with it. Sleep with it before you on your curtains. "Thou God seest me!"

> O may this thought possess my breast,
> Where'er I rove, where'er I rest;
> Nor let my weaker passions dare
> Consent to sin, for God is there!

The Heavy Tidings

The woman stood amazed as the prophet proceeded to expose the iniquity of her husband's house, the certain judgment that God would execute, and the terrible disgrace with which the name of Jeroboam should be execrated because they had revolted from God and set up for themselves the calves of Baal. As for the child, respecting whom she had come to inquire, he would die. That death was the quenching of a bright spark in the heart of the parents, but nonetheless a mercy for the youth. "All Israel shall mourn for him, and bury him: for he only of Jeroboam shall come to the grave, because in him there is found some good thing toward the LORD God of Israel in the house of Jeroboam" (1 Kings 14:13).

Let me linger on this part of the narrative a moment. In that wicked house there was one bright gem upon which the Lord put a high value. The lad was taken from the evil to come. The kindness of the Lord appeared in his death, while all the judgments were reserved for his father's family. Do I not speak to some of you ungodly persons who have lost your little children? While you wept bitter tears as you carried them to the grave, you said, "Well, he is better off"; or, "She sleeps in Jesus?" Did you never think, that as for you, you are worse off? You have no hope and are living without God in the world.

Let us picture Jeroboam and his wife at the tent of their son, Abijah. There was everything to cheer the heart as to him who had departed, but everything to fill the soul with gloom concerning those who remained. The like has been the case at the funerals of your gracious little ones. We need shed no tears over the bier. Let us keep our lamentations for the mourners who attend the funeral. Ah! but you may make the reflections all your own. You, too, have been outside the gates of the city to carry your offspring to the spot in God's acre where they now slumber. Did you think in that mournful hour that the firstfruits of your household was holy to the Lord? We never cease to wonder that the young should die. Yet it has ever been so. Well indeed can I believe that mercy of a sweet-smelling savor is to be found in those dispensations of God's providence that so often darken the windows of our heart and wither the fairest buds in our garden.

Where of old did death strike its first dart? Did it pierce the heart of Adam the sinner, or smite down the relentless Cain? No, but righteous Abel was the first of men who departed from earth, to be absent from the body and present with the Lord. Even so have you, full many of you, committed your children to the dust, in an assured hope for them, according to the Word of the Lord; a hope that you cannot cherish for yourselves. O sinners, be chary of your tears, your sighs, and your groans. Pour them not out with such profuseness as a libation at the graves of those who sleep in Jesus and are blest. You will need them all for your own souls presently. Take up a lamentation for your own doom. Except you repent, your funerals, O ungodly ones, will call for shrill notes of endless despair.

Let me pause. I have glad tidings to preach to some of you before I yet again deliver these heavy tidings to those who despise the Word.

Is there one soul here that desires to be saved? Sinner, I have glad tidings for you. Here are the words: "Whosoever will, let him take the water of life freely" (Rev. 22:17). Though you have been a drunkard or a swearer, though you have been a whoremonger or a thief, yet there is salvation for any man who comes to Jesus Christ for it. And if the Spirit of God moves you to come now,

> Let not conscience make you linger;
>   Nor of fitness fondly dream:
> All the fitness he requireth,
>   Is to feel your need of him:
> This he gives you;
> 'Tis his Spirit's rising beam.

You say, "How can I go to Christ?" It is no great effort. It is in fact the absence of all effort. You have not to climb to heaven to reach Him, nor to travel to the ends of the earth to find Him. Never doubt, if the Holy Spirit be with you, you may find Him tonight. The way to be saved is simply to trust Christ. Jesus Christ took the guilt of His people and carried it himself. If you trust Him, you shall have peace, for Jesus took your sin. An old servant was once carrying a large bough of a tree to have it cut into pieces to make a fire. A little boy, one of the family, seeing the end of it dragging along the ground and making it very heavy, came and took hold of the end and the burden grew light. Then said the servant, "Ah! master Frank, I wish you could take hold of one end of the greater burden that I have to carry. I have a burden of sin. The more I drag it about, the heavier it becomes. I wish Jesus Christ would take hold of one end of it." The little boy said,

"My mother told me yesterday that Jesus Christ carries all our sins. Therefore, you do not want Jesus Christ to drag one end of it, He will take the whole of it." The poor woman, who had been long seeking rest, found it by that remark of the child. Yes, Jesus does take your sins. If you trust Christ, this is the evidence that all your sins are laid on Him.

> Sinner, nothing do,
> Either great or small;
> Jesus did it, did it all,
> Long, long ago.

Your salvation is finished by Christ if you believe. Not only the first strokes, but the finishing touch Christ has given. The bath you shall wash in, He has filled it. The robe you shall wear, He has woven it. The crown you shall wear, He has bought it. The heaven you shall inhabit, He has prepared it. "It is finished" (John 19:30). All you have to do is to wear it. Take it and wear it. Accept it as a gift of His free grace. May God bring you into such a mind that you may be willing to receive it. And if you are willing so to receive it, take it—take it and go your way rejoicing. Thus you see, I bring good tidings to seekers.

But I have a heavy message for some of you. Let me deliver it in the sight of God with deep solemnity of purpose. Sinner, unrepenting sinner, I have heavy tidings for you. You are now under God's wrath. The wrath of God abides on you. It is not as though a tempest hovered in the sky. It has gathered around your devoted head! "God is angry with the wicked every day" (Ps. 7:11). Sinner, God has bent his bow, made it ready, and fitted His arrow to the string, and He has pointed it at you. He has furbished His sword and made it sharp. It is sharp for you. O barren fig tree, the ax is laid at your root! God even now looks upon you with anger as you offend against Him, and sin with a high hand. Turn! Turn! For it is either turn or burn! May God get you to turn lest you burn forever. I have worse tidings still, as you will think. There is speedy death for you. I know not how long you may live, but out of this vast assembly there is every probability that one or two of us will be in eternity before next Sunday. You can calculate that as well as I can.

There is a certain number of deaths in the population every week. Here are several thousands gathered here—some six or seven thousand immortal souls. We may die, but there are some of us who *must* die. It is rarely a week passes without a death of someone in this church, much more in the congregation. I suppose I never did address the same assembly twice, and never shall. Though you were all willing to come next Sunday, yet there will be some of you who could not come because you will have appeared at the bar of God. Prepare to meet your God. There is no cholera abroad, but death has other weapons. The fever sleeps, but the gates to the grave are many. You may pass through one of them before you are ever aware of it. Prepare! Prepare, because He will do this. "Prepare to meet thy God, O Israel" (Amos 4:12). I have heavy tidings for some of you. I give you warning to set your house in order, for you must die and not live. I speak now prophetically of some here present. Let them take heed to their ways lest the day of grace pass and they die before they have thought of Christ.

I have heavier tidings still. After death the judgment. First comes the skeleton king, and then hell follows him. Oh! is it true that some of us may be in hell before another week? True! alas! too true! I do conjure you then—since there is this possibility. No, since there is an absolute certainty that before long, except we repent, we shall all likewise perish—I do conjure you think upon your eternal state. By the wrath of God and by the love of God, by your own soul and by the value of it, by heaven and its joys which you will lose, by hell and its torments which you must endure, by the blood of Jesus, by the groans and sweat of that Redeemer who delights to receive sinners and who declares that any who come to Him He will in no wise cast out. I pray you, as your brother and your friend, fly, fly, fly to Jesus! May the Lord help you to trust Him now. There, just as you are, flat before the cross, sinner, no stopping, no waiting, no preparing. Come to Jesus all in your dishabille, all black and filthy, just as you are. "Mercy's gate is never shut, Jesus' heart is never hard." His blood shall never lose its power. Do trust Him, trust Him, trust Him, and we will meet in heaven to praise His name, world without end. Amen.

NOTES

Enoch: Walking with God

George H. Morrison (1866–1928) assisted the great Alexander Whyte in Edinburgh, pastored two churches, and then, in 1902, became pastor of the distinguished Wellington Church on University Avenue in Glasgow, Scotland. His preaching drew great crowds; in fact, people had to line up an hour before the services to ensure that they got seats in the large auditorium. Morrison was a master of imagination in preaching, yet his messages are solidly biblical.

From his many published volumes of sermons, I have chosen this message, found in *The World-Wide Gospel*, published in 1933 by Hodder and Stoughton, London.

GEORGE H. MORRISON

6

Enoch: Walking with God

And Enoch walked with God. (Genesis 5:22)

THIS CHAPTER IS AN uninterrupted record of the generations from Adam to the Deluge. It is a monotonous chronicle of nobodies. One after another they deploy before us a moment visible then gone forever. The only memorial they have left is that they were born and begat children and died. And it is in the midst of that long and dreary list, without one touch of human interest in it, that suddenly we light on this: "And Enoch walked with God." Like the song of a caged bird heard unexpectedly through all the hurrying of a city street or like a rowan tree, red with berries, that has rooted on some naked cliff, so in the midst of this expanse of names comes this touch of music and of color. "And Enoch walked with God." What kind of life he lived we cannot tell. Of his trials and his triumphs we know nothing. His occupation, his intellectual abilities—such things are hidden from our eyes. The one lasting impression Enoch made, the one that swallowed up all other memories, was that here had been a man who walked with God.

How that impression, which must have been very powerful when it obliterated every other memory, was created, the Scripture does not tell us. A well-known German writer of religious allegories has one that goes somewhat in this fashion. He tells of a villager who, wherever he went, was accompanied by an unseen friend. When he entered a room he stepped aside to let his invisible companion enter first. When he sat at the table an extra place was set, and the choicest bits were put on the other plate. When he was dying there was a chair beside his bed, and someone invisible was sitting on it with whom he talked in whispers until he died. Such a man did not mount up with wings. There was nothing soaring or sublime about him. But what everybody felt was that he walked with an invisible companion. And the deepest impression of the life of Enoch, absorbing every other memory, was that Enoch too had walked with the unseen.

"Tell me the secret of your life," said one to Kingsley. Kingsley replied, "I had a friend." And that was the secret of the life of Enoch. He too, like Kingsley, had a friend—One whom he talked with every day he lived, One who was intensely real to him, One with whom he shared the sorrows that came to Enoch as they come to all. I asked a young friend the other day if he prayed, and he told me that he sometimes prayed. He told me he had to undergo an operation lately, and he prayed very earnestly that morning. But Enoch did not pray on special mornings. He trusted, prayed, conquered every morning, until at last men felt with a great certainty that Enoch walked with God. There was a beautiful serenity about him that the world could neither give nor take away. There was the wisdom that is from above, that is pure, peaceable, easy to be entreated. Enoch was in the world and yet not of the world. They saw he had meat to eat they knew not of. So when he passed away this was their memory, that "Enoch walked with God." They used to say of Dante in the streets of Florence, "There goes the man who has seen hell." I sometimes see faces in our Glasgow streets that recall that whispering of the Florentines. But no one said that of Enoch. His life was so calm, so beautiful, so spiritual, they said of him, "Enoch walked with God."

My brother and sister, have you ever seriously thought of the ultimate impression which your life will make? It is a question that is well worth considering. When the smoke is hanging on the field of battle it is difficult to tell how the fight goes. There are swift movements, then sudden attacks, repulses here and shouts of triumph yonder. And yet through all the confusion and the cloud, the battle is making for one issue, and by that issue shall it be remembered. Few of us know the tactics of Flodden, yet we all know it was a terrible defeat. Few know the management of Waterloo, yet we all know it was a glorious victory. And the question that I want you to consider is, What will be the verdict on your life when the clouds have lifted and the strife is over and after these voices there is peace? Will it be that you have lived a useless life? God grant that the final impression be not that. Happy he who when it all is over has a verdict given him like that of Enoch.

Enoch's Life Was Deepened by Experience

There are three suggestions about Enoch in these verses that are worthwhile calling to your notice. The first is how his life was deepened by experience. Will you read the verse that precedes our text? It tells us that Enoch "lived" for sixty-five years. Not "walked with God," you observe, for sixty-five years, but "lived" for sixty–five years like all the others. And then his son was born, his firstborn son, and the life of Enoch was deepened into fatherhood. And now for the first time we read that Enoch walked with God. One of our Scottish ministers who died some twenty years ago left a diary that has since been printed. It is a beautiful record of a beautiful soul. Well, one of the entries in that diary is this (and I have never forgotten it since I first read it): "I never see my little child playing on the rug before the fire, but I hear God saying to me, 'Thou art forgiven.'" Now think of Enoch, who was the seventh from Adam, and try to picture what God meant to him. Think of all he must have learned in boyhood of the Fall and the anger of heaven and the Curse. And then his child was born and life was deepened for him, and love on earth spoke of a love in heaven—"And Enoch walked with God."

My brother, is it not touches such as that that bring all the ages into unity? How often religion becomes real at last through the heightening and deepening of experience! Trained in the atmosphere of Christian homes, we cling to the simple habits of our childhood. We believe in God, we pray, we come to church, yet religion has never been very real to us. Then life is deepened—sometimes in an hour, sometimes through a more gradual experience—and we begin to feel our utter need of God. Prayer becomes real; sin becomes abhorrent. We feel our need of a great pardoning mercy. Promises that once were idle words now ring for us with the music of high heaven. That is what experience can do. That is what death can do. That is what joy and sorrow in the home can do—taking the average life of Enoch and deepening it into a walk with God.

Enoch Walked with God in Very Evil Times

The second thing to be observed is this, that Enoch walked with God in very evil times. These days before the flood, as the next chapter tells us, were days of fearful wickedness. Men had cast the fear of God from them and had become utterly corrupt. Men had descended to the level of the beast, and lawlessness and violence were everywhere. And amid all that riot and rebellion, all that forgetfulness of what was pure and beautiful, Enoch walked with God. There was everything in that age to drag him down. There was little in that age to lift him up. Men had forgotten God before the flood came, and God had given them over to their lusts. And amid all that sin and violence Enoch walked, serene and beautiful and calm and pure, in the daily fellowship of the invisible.

I do not need to tell you what an influence a life like that would wield. You know that without any words of mine. We do not know if Enoch preached—we have no hint given us of his occupation—but how Enoch lived in the long period of years that God allotted him, and how a life like that would tell, when everywhere there was indifference and ungodliness, you know as well as I do. There are certain arguments that serve their day and then become obsolete or antiquated. There are proofs that are powerful with one age and are practically powerless with the next. But there is one proof that is never antiquated and never loses its power of appeal, and that is the proof of the man who walks with God. It is easy, it is always easy, to deny the inspiration of a book. But the one thing men can never do is to deny the inspiration of a life. And when that life through ever-lengthening years is calm and beautiful and wise and blameless, it wins a power over the hearts of men with which nothing on earth can be compared. "And Enoch walked with God." Can you not picture how men would turn to him in times of perplexity and difficulty? Can you not conceive how they would trust him and feel themselves honored by his friendship! Steadfast and stable, old yet ever young, tender of heart and of a blameless character, the life of Enoch did more for God and glory than the preaching of a thousand sermons.

Enoch Walked with God upon the Common Round

Then the third point to be observed is this: Enoch walked with God upon the common round. He was not hurried away into solitude after the birth of his firstborn. He "walked with God . . . and begat sons and daughters" (v. 22), says our passage. That means that he still lived at home. He did not leave his dwelling or his wife or the dull duties of ordinary days. He took up his cross daily in his dwelling, did his day's work, played with his growing children, yet everyone saw that a change had come to Enoch, for once he had only lived, and now he walked with God. Enoch walked with God among his family. That is the most striking feature in the story. It is so utterly different from what we should have expected in any record of these primeval times. For you all know that in these primeval times to be holy, to be separated were identical, and yet Enoch walked with God and was not separated. He begat children and he lived at home. It was a far-off glimpse of that coming age when on the bells of the horses was to be written holiness. Enoch, like Abraham, saw the day of Christ, and seeing it was glad. Not in great tasks that drove him into solitude, but in the common round and in his home. That is the wonder of it, that in this earliest narrative we should be told that Enoch walked with God.

And so the piety of Enoch is the piety to which you and I are called. Do you seek great things for yourself? Seek them not. It has been said that the mark of a true Christian is not to do extraordinary things. The mark of a true Christian is to do ordinary things in an extraordinary way. To bring the highest to bear upon the least, to interpenetrate with heaven the daily duty, may be a better witness to a living Christ than that a man should give his body to be burned. "Though I speak with the tongues of men and of angels, and have not charity . . . it profiteth me nothing" (1 Cor. 13:1–3). And how does charity reveal itself? The New Testament will answer that. Charity suffers long and is kind. Charity is not easily provoked. Charity bears all things, believes all things, hopes all things. That was how Enoch walked with God, and that is how we know nothing of it all. There was nothing heroic in it, nothing splendid, nothing magnificent in deed or sacrifice. He lived at home and the little children came, and the joys and sorrows of the dwelling touched him. Enoch did quite ordinary things, but he did them in an extraordinary way.

Enoch saw the hand of God in everything. There was no such thing as chance in Enoch's home. He was always praying, always asking guidance, always because God was there. Long before David wrote his noble psalm, Enoch had cast his burden on the Lord and found daily that the Lord sustained him. Such a life as that was bound to tell, and this dull chapter shows us how it told. Silently, through unrecorded years, one deep definite impression was created. And so when Enoch was taken home to glory, men did not say he was erudite or brilliant, but with love and reverence in their hearts they said, "Enoch walked with God." It takes long years to give that certainty. It is not created in a day. Sorrow and joy and suffering and toil it takes, from youth, through manhood, into age. But when at last in the midst of common life men become conscious of it as a living fact, it helps and blesses them to the last hour they live and makes God and heaven very real. To have known anyone who walked with God is to have had one of the highest privileges on earth. It is a memory that will never fail us when troubles come and when the shadows deepen. And if to us this morning there come such a memory, let us remember before it be too late, that to "whomsoever much is given, of him shall be much required" (Luke 12:48).

Simon Magus

Alexander Whyte (1836–1921) was known as "the last of the Puritans," and certainly his sermons were surgical as he magnified the glory of God and exposed the depravity of sin. He succeeded the noted Robert S. Candlish as pastor of Free Saint George's and reigned from that influential Edinburgh pulpit for nearly forty years. He loved to "dig again in the old wells" and share with his people truths learned from the devotional masters of the past. His evening Bible courses attracted the young people and led many into a deeper walk with God.

This sermon was taken from *Bible Characters from the Old and New Testaments,* reprinted in 1990 by Kregel Publications.

ALEXANDER WHYTE

7

Simon Magus

Acts 8:9–25

But who, to begin with, was Simon Magus? And how did it come about that he believed and was actually baptized by Philip the evangelist, and then was detected, denounced, and utterly reprobated by the apostle Peter? How did all that come about?

Well, you must know that Samaria, where Simon Magus lived and carried on his astounding impositions, was a half-Hebrew, half-heathen country. Samaria had just enough of the Hebrew blood in its veins to make it full of the very worst qualities of that blood, mixed up with some of the very worst qualities of the heathen blood of that day also. And Simon Magus was at once the natural product and the divine punishment of that apostate land in which we find him living in such mountebank prosperity. Simon Magus was a very clever man and, at the same time, a very bad man, until, by his tremendous pretensions, he had the whole of Samaria at his feet. There was something positively sublime about the impudence and charlatanry of Simon Magus, until he was actually feared and obeyed and worshiped as nothing short of some divinity who had condescended to come and take up his abode in Samaria. But the whole man and the whole situation is best set before us in the two or three strokes of the sacred writer:

> There was a certain man, called Simon, which beforetime in the same city used sorcery, and bewitched the people of Samaria, giving out that himself was some great one. To whom they all gave heed, from the least to the greatest, saying, This man is the great power of God. And to him they had regard, because that of long time he had bewitched them with sorceries. But when they believed Philip preaching the things concerning the kingdom of God, and the name of Jesus Christ, they were baptized, both men and women. Then Simon himself believed also: and when he was baptized, he continued with Philip, and wondered, beholding the miracles and signs which were done. (Acts 8:9–13)

Philip had extraordinary success in his evangelizing mission to Samaria. It was like New England, or Cambuslang, or 1859–1860, or Moody and Sankey's first visit to Scotland. For the people with one accord gave heed to those things that Philip spoke, hearing and seeing the miracles that he did. And there was great joy in that city. "The very devil himself has been converted and has been baptized by me," Philip telegraphed to Jerusalem. "I actually have the name of Simon Magus on my communion roll." At the hearing of that, the apostles sent two of their foremost men down to Samaria to superintend the great movement, and God sent the Holy Spirit with them, until the whole of Samaria seemed to have turned to God and to the name of Jesus Christ. Only Simon Magus was all the time such an impostor that in his conversation and baptism he had completely deceived Philip. No, I think it but fair to Simon Magus to say that he had completely deceived himself as well as Philip. I think so. I am bound in charity to think so.

When Simon Magus came up out of the water, had a voice from heaven spoken at that moment, it would surely have been heard to say, "This is an arch-deceiver, deceiving, but, at the same time, being deceived." Some men have far more self-discernment than other men, and self-discernment is the highest and the rarest science of all the sciences on the face of the earth. And, usually, there is united with great self-discernment, and as a reward and a premium put by God upon its exercise, the power of deeply discerning other men's spirits also. Now, although Philip was a prince of evangelistic preachers, and a good and an able man, at the same time he was far too easily satisfied with his converts. Philip was far better at preaching than he was at catechizing. And thus it was that it fell to Peter and John to purge Philip's communion roll of Simon Magus immediately on their arrival in Samaria. At the same time, this must be said, that Simon Magus had never come out in his true colors until after Peter's arrival, and until after all the true converts had received the Holy Spirit.

The circumstances were these: It was part of the Pentecostal equipment of the apostles to possess for a time some of the miracle-working powers that their divine Master had exercised in order to arrest attention to His advent, and to secure a hearing to His ministry. And thus it is that we find the apostles speaking with tongues, healing the sick, opening the eyes of the blind, casting out devils, and many suchlike miracles and signs. Now Simon Magus, like everybody else in Samaria, was immensely impressed with all that he saw and heard. No man was more impressed than Simon Magus, or more convinced of the divine mission of the apostles. But with all his wonder and with all his conviction, he was never truly converted. The love of money, and the still more intoxicating love of notoriety, had taken such absolute possession of Simon Magus that he simply could not live out of the eyes of men. He must be in men's mouths. He must have a crowd around him.

Themistocles could not sleep because of the huzzahs that filled the streets of Athens when Miltiades walked abroad. The crowds that followed Peter and John were gall and wormwood to Simon Magus. For still greater crowds used to take him up and carry him on their shoulders in the days of his great power before Philip came to Samaria. Now Peter had never liked the look of

Philip's great convert, and it completely justified Peter's incurable suspicions when Simon Magus came one night into Peter's lodgings and, setting down a bag of money on the table, said, "What will you take for the Holy Ghost? If you will show me the secret of your apostleship so that I may work your miracles like you, I have plenty of money, and I know where there is plenty more." The sight of the bag and the blasphemous proposal of the owner of the bag nearly drove Peter beside himself. And the old fisherman so blazed out at the poor mountebank that the page burns red to this day with Peter's denunciation: "Thy money perish with thee. . . . For I perceive that thou art in the gall of bitterness, and in the bond of iniquity" (vv. 20, 23).

"Giving out that himself was some great one" (v. 9). That is our first lesson from this Holy Scripture about Simon Magus. Let those take the lesson to heart who specially need it, and who will humble themselves to receive it. It may be sorcery and witchcraft like that of Simon Magus. It may be in the honors of the kingdom of heaven like the sons of Zebedee. It may be in preaching sermons. It may be in making speeches or writing books. It may be in anything you like, down to your children's possessions and performances. But we all, to begin with, give ourselves out to be some great one. Simon Magus was but an exaggerated specimen of every popularity hunter among us. There is an element and first principle of Simon Magus, the Samaritan mountebank, in all public men. There is still a certain residuum of Simon left in order to his last sanctification in every minister. But the most Simon Magus-like of all sanctified ministers I know is Thomas Shepard, and that just because he is the most self-discerning, the most honest, and the most outspoken about himself of us all. Popularity was the very breath of life to that charlatan of Samaria. He could not work, he could not live, he could not be converted and baptized, without popularity. And there is not one public man in a thousand, politician or preacher, who will go on living and working and praying out of sight, and all the time with sweetness, contentment, goodwill, and a quiet heart.

All Samaria must give heed to Simon Magus from the least to the greatest. And so still with his successors. A despairing missionary to the drunken navvies on a new railway complained to me the other day that one of our great preachers, who was there on holiday in the neighborhood, would not give an idle Sabbath afternoon hour to the men loitering about the door. It was the dregs of Simon Magus in the city orator. He could not kindle but to a crowd. "Seek obscurity" was Fénelon's motto. Whether he lived up to his motto or not, the day will declare. If he did, there will not be many wearing the same crown with him on that day. But Richard Baxter will be one of them.

> I am much less regardful of the approbation of men, and set much lighter by contempt or applause, than I did long ago. All worldly things appear most vain and unsatisfactory when we have tried them most. But though I feel that this hath some hand in the effect, yet the knowledge of man's nothingness, and of God's transcendent greatness, with whom it is that I have most to do, and the sense of the brevity of human things, and the nearness of eternity, are the principal causes of this effect, and not self-conceitedness and morosity, as some suppose.

These things will help to do it, but above all these things a completely broken heart will alone cast Simon Magus out of us ministers. A heart broken beyond all mollification or binding up in this world, but not even a broken heart, unless it is daily broken. Nothing will root the mountebank out of us ministers but constant self-detection, constant self-contempt, constant self-denunciation, and constant self-destruction. Oh, my friends, you do not know, and you are not fit to be told, the tremendous price of a minister's salvation. It is this that makes our crucified Master say to us ministers continually, "Few there be that find it" (Matt. 7:14).

You will not know what a "law-work" is, but Simon Magus was simply lost for want of a law-work. You never nowadays hear the once universal pulpit word. The Romans and the Galatians are full of the law-work, and so have all our greatest preachers been. Those two great evangelical Epistles were not yet written, but there was enough of their contents in the Pentecostal air, if Simon Magus had had any taste for such soul-searching matters. I must not allow myself to say a single word as to Philip's mismanagement of his catechumens' and young communicants' classes. Only the sorcerer must have sadly bewitched the evangelist before Philip put Simon Magus's name down on his communion roll. Philip knew his business and his own heart. I dare not doubt that. Only, somehow or other, he let Simon Magus slip through his hands much too easily. Believing, baptism, communion table, and all, Simon Magus had neither part nor lot in this matter of the work of the law. I would not keep either a young communicant or an old convert away from the table because he was not deeply learned in all the Pauline doctrines. But I could not undertake to recommend his name to the kirk-session unless he gave me some evidence of what the masters of our science call the law-work. He might never have heard the word, and I would never mention it to him unless, indeed, he was a man of some mind. But it is mocking God and deluding men to crowd the table with communicants like Simon Magus who do not know the first principles either of sin or of salvation. The best law-work comes to us long after conversion and admission to the table. But neither before his so-called conversion, nor after it, did this arch-impostor know anything about it—"for thy heart," said Peter, tearing it open to its very core, "is not right in the sight of God" (Acts 8:21).

"Fictus," that is to say, a living and breathing fiction, was the name given to such converts as Simon Magus in those early days. Ignorance, Temporary, Pliable, and Turnaway were some of their names in later days. Now you are not an impostor by profession like Simon Magus. You do not make your living by deluding other people. But there may very easily be an element of fiction, of self-delusion and self-imposition, in your supposed conversion as there was in his. Calvin's moderation, saneness of judgment, and spiritual insight carry me with him here also. "I am not of their mind," he says, "who think that Simon Magus made only a semblance of religion. There is a middle ground between saving faith and sheer dissimulation. Simon Magus saw that the apostles' doctrine was true, and he received the same so far. But the groundwork was all along wanting—that is to say, his denial of himself was all along wanting."

Just so. I see and feel Calvin's point. Your religion is not all a sham on your part. You are not a pure and unmixed hypocrite. But neither is your religion of the right kind. It is not saving your soul. It is not making you every day a new and another man. Your heart is not right in the sight of God. It is not and never will be until, as Calvin says and as Christ says, you deny yourself daily. And that, every day, to your heart's blood and in the matter of the sin that so easily besets you. With Simon Magus it was the praise of men and their crowding around him and their adulation of him. Now what he should have done, and what Philip should have insisted on him to do, was to discover to himself and to confess to himself his besetting sin, and every day to drive another nail of self-crucifixion into it. Another new nail every day until it gave up the ghost. Instead of that the poor impostor tried to get Peter to share his apostolic popularity with him for thirty pieces of silver! If you are a platform, a pulpit, or any other kind of mountebank, seek obscurity, for your soul's salvation lies there. If you are a popular preacher, flee from crowded churches and hold services in huts, poorhouses, and barns, and kitchens. Never search the papers to see what they are saying about you. Starve the self-seeking quack that is still within you. Beat him black and blue, as Paul tells us he did, and as Thomas Shepard tells us he did, every time he shows his self-admiring face.

Simon Magus put the thought of his heart into the form of a money proposal to Peter. But, bad as the proposal was, it was not much the proposal that Peter so struck at as the heart of the proposer: "If perhaps the thought of thine heart may be forgiven thee" (v. 22). Now answer this, as we shall all answer it one day: What about the thoughts of your heart? Are the self-seeking, self-exalting thoughts of your heart dwelt on and indulged, or are they the greatest shame to you and the greatest torment to you of your life? Do you hate your own heart as you would hate hell itself if you were about to be cast down into it? Do you beat your breast and cry out, Oh, wretched man that I am! Has the law entered and is the law-work deep enough and spiritual enough to make all the Simon Magus-like thoughts of your hearts to be an inward pain and shame to you past all knowledge, and past all belief about you, of mortal man? His thoughts, that is, of self-advertisement, self-exaltation, and self-congratulation? Does the praise of men puff you up and make you very happy? And is their silence or their absence something you cannot get over? Is he a good man who follows you about and believes in you and applauds you? Is he an unpardonably bad man who prefers Philip, Peter, and John to Simon Magus? Then, be not deceived, God is not mocked and neither are the self-discerning men around you. Both your happiness and your sadness, both your love and your hatred of men are quite naked and open to those with whom you have to do: "For I perceive that thou art still in the gall of bitterness, and in the bond of iniquity." "We may conjecture," says Calvin, "that Simon Magus repented." Whereas Bengel leaves it to the last day to discover that and to declare that.

NOTES

Esau: The Profane

George Campbell Morgan (1863–1945) was the son of a British Baptist preacher and preached his first sermon when he was thirteen years old. He had no formal training for the ministry, but his tireless devotion to the study of the Bible helped him to become one of the leading Bible teachers of his day. Rejected by the Methodists, he was ordained into the Congregational ministry. He was associated with Dwight L. Moody in the Northfield Bible conferences and as an itinerant Bible teacher. He is best known as the pastor of the Westminster Chapel, London (1904–1917 and 1933–1943). During his second term there, he had Dr. D. Martyn Lloyd-Jones as his associate.

Morgan published more than sixty books and booklets, and his sermons are found in *The Westminster Pulpit* (London: Hodder and Stoughton, 1906–1916). This sermon was taken from *26 Sermons by Dr. G. Campbell Morgan,* volume 3, published 1969 by College Press, Joplin, Missouri, in the Evangelical Reprint Library series.

8

Esau: The Profane

Genesis 25:27–34; 1 Corinthians 1:1–2; 3:16–18; 6:19–20

Esau despised his birthright. (Genesis 25:34)

Profane person, as Esau, who for one morsel of meat sold his birthright. (Hebrews 12:16)

It is written that Isaac loved Esau, and we immediately sympathize with him. It is also written that God hated Esau, and we wonder and question and very often attempt to explain away the statement.

Isaac we perfectly understand and his love of Esau we understand. Esau was preeminently a lovable man—strong and healthy; a man of the open air, the field, and the woods; a keen sportsman, genial and generous, utterly unable to cherish resentment or to carry it out in spite of his own threats. Study the story of this man as he crosses the pages of this ancient history, and it is impossible to escape from these impressions. I repeat, we understand Isaac's love for him.

What then shall we say in the presence of the declaration so strange, "Jacob have I loved, but Esau have I hated" (Rom. 9:13), the awful word of God concerning this man?

Let us make another affirmation. We know God by revelation and by faith, and the knowledge we have of God convinces us that the Judge of all the earth must do right, that His judgments are righteous judgments, that His verdicts are true verdicts, and that against His sentence there can be no appeal. Notwithstanding the fact that our observation of this man in the ordinary things of everyday life is one that brings us into sympathy with Isaac in his love of him; it is important and necessary that we should attempt to see him from the height of the divine viewpoint. That is the key to the situation. If there be no heaven above and no God enthroned and no large, spiritual issue of all the fleeting hours and material things, then Esau is wholly admirable. But immediately we realize the true viewpoint and begin to look at this man from the standard of God's observation, we are arrested by the word that the writer of the letter to the Hebrews used concerning him. We recognize at once that it is fitting and revealing, "that profane person Esau."

Let us refresh our memories as to the incidents recorded concerning this man. First, we are told that the boys grew. While Jacob was a quiet, peaceful man by nature, living the life of the tents and among the flocks, Esau was a cunning hunter, a man of the field; failing to recognize the responsibilities of home, and giving himself to a wilder manner of life that had in it no necessary vulgarity, but which nevertheless was the life of irresponsibility.

Then we have the picture of the passage I read this evening, central in the story of this man's spiritual nature and career, the selling of the birthright. Coming in from the fields faint and hungry, seeing the red pottage, he clamored for it and said, Give me of that red!

I am not this evening dealing with Jacob. We have done that in a previous sermon. That Jacob should take advantage of Esau's hunger was dastardly and mean. But that a man should allow himself to be taken advantage of in such a matter as that, compels us to consider him in the loneliness of his own personal choice and volition.

The third picture that we have as we turn over the pages of this book of Genesis is that of him as he went out and took two daughters of the Canaanite people as his wives, Judith and Basemath. There is no hint of anything unworthy in his attitude toward these daughters of the land. He did not trifle with them. He did not betray them. There is no suggestion that in after years he ill-treated them. But he answered the appeal of his own nature without reference to principle.

The next picture of the man is of him returning after Jacob's deceit with the venison for which his father had clamored. We see him crying for the blessing that he had sold.

Then almost immediately afterward we see him acting upon some sudden impulse or desire to be in some measure pleasing to his parents. When Jacob had been sent away to find a wife of his own people, we see Esau compromising and taking again a wife. This time in the person of the daughter of Ishmael.

The last picture that has any particular significance is that of Esau meeting Jacob as he returned after twenty years of sojourning in the land of Laban. Esau meets Jacob generously, absolutely forgetting the wrong done in the past. When Jacob settled in the land of Canaan, Esau gathered his people, cattle, and property together and resolutely and for the last time parted company with the land and took up his abode in Seir.

There is one other picture in which we see him side by side with Jacob committing to rest the ashes of his father Isaac.

These are all the pictures of the man that we get in the book of Genesis. None of them are very full, and there is not a single one, I venture to affirm, that startles the conscience. After telling how he gave his birthright to Jacob for a mess of pottage, the writer adds this pregnant phrase, "Esau despised his birthright." Yet that phrase may be read in assemblies such as this over and over again and awaken no sense of shame or fear. We have a sort of subconscious idea that there was something improper and irreligious in the action. But we all have in the underworld of our human nature some kind of regard and respect for Esau.

I turn over to the letter to the Hebrews and read the account of the men and women of the past who were heroes and heroines of faith—men who "endured, as seeing him who is invisible" (Heb. 11:27), women who "judged him faithful who had promised" (v. 11), and people who saw visions that other people did not see, and who made great renunciations in order that all the strength of life might be put into the business of translating vision into victory. When I am through with the story of the heroes and heroines of faith, I find the writer of the letter to the Hebrews warning against the possibility of apostasy, the turning of the back upon the same principle of faith. When he is culminating his warning, making it vivid and terrific, he quotes this man, "Lest there be any fornicator, or profane person, as Esau, who for one morsel of meat sold his birthright" (12:16).

The word thus stamped upon this story is the word *profane*. Yet there is nothing to suggest profanity in our ordinary acceptation of the word. We might have said of Peter, That profane person, Peter. On one occasion, under stress of temptation, mastered by cowardice, he cursed and swore that he did not know his Lord. That is what we call profanity. We pass down the street where such men live, and thank God we are not as they are. That man profanely swearing upon the highway may not be profane according to the measurements of heaven, while the man who despises him may be entirely profane; for the balances of the sanctuary are not the balances of humanity, and the measurements of God are not the measurements of man. It is important that we should look at this man from that viewpoint, and see him weighed in the balances of the sanctuary.

Let us try to find out what this means. Our word *profane* is in some senses the equivalent translation of the word used by the writer of the letter to the Hebrews, but I prefer to find out what word he used. I am almost startled and mystified when I commence my examination by discovering that the word this writer used about Esau is a word that literally means "to walk the threshold." That does not seem to help us very much. It seems as though we have gone out of the realm of things serious. To walk the threshold—that is the fundamental meaning of the word that is translated *profane*. Our word *profane* simply means outside the sanctuary, before the fane, but not of it. That, however, misses the tremendous revelation of the actual word which the writer used. That "profane person," is that threshold trampled person! What does that mean? The door wide open. And what does that mean? Accessible. That accessible person Esau; that person who had no reserve in his nature, no sense of responsibility, no holy of holies. Every gate was open, every avenue of his being was a highway across which every vagrant emotion and unholy passion might march and counter march.

Did not the apostle say—and the meaning of my reading of the passages in the Corinthian letter is now self-evident—"Know ye not that your body is the temple of the Holy Ghost?" (1 Cor. 6:19). The word here translated *temple* is not one which would describe the whole temple in Jerusalem, it is a word that described the inner sanctuary, the holy of holies. "Know ye not that your body is a holy of holies of the Holy Ghost," the very sanctuary of God, its gates closed against all that would insult His holiness, deny His love, or be contrary to His government. Esau was a profane person—simply a man with all the gateways of his being open, mastered now by emotion, presently by passion, a little later by lust, now by greed, and anon by generosity. A tenantless house, a shrine without a deity, a man without a master-principle. That "profane person Esau."

Look back at the incidents of his life. This was manifest in his youth. He was a man of the field and given over to sport; a man who had lost his sense of responsibility.

Look at the hour of the birthright sale. The immediate passion of hunger entered in and mastered him, and he was prepared to barter anything to answer the hunger of the moment.

There came a day when the daughters of the land of Canaan made appeal to his nature and he immediately took them. He was honorable in his dealing with them to all human seeming. But forgetting the principle involved in his very blood and life as a man of the chosen people of God, not reckoning with these things, not mastered by any religious principle, he acted in answer to that appeal.

When, in after years, he came back and found that the blessing had been filched from him by the meanness of his brother, he clamored, not for the high and holy rights involved in the birthright blessing, but for some blessing, some advantage for himself.

Presently there passed through his nature some spasm of desire toward higher things, and he indulged it by compromising with principle, as he married the daughter of Ishmael.

After a while, generous to a fault in regard to his brother when he came home, he was yet perfectly prepared to abandon all connection with that race to which he was related by blood, and to take all his property and settle in Seir.

In every incident we find a new reason, a new passion, a new motive, a profane person, a temple with the doors open and all the unhallowed crowds tramping in and out, walking across the threshold. There is no sanctity, no sacredness, no reserve, no consciousness of high and holy things, no recognition of principle, no sense of responsibility.

How many of us see our own portraits? No vulgar sin as yet has blackened our escutcheon; nothing to which this age of the near, this present age to which Demas turned, will take objection; nothing that this age will condemn; but profane, in that we have desire without direction, which we answer on the spur of the moment; pleasure without principle, and we sell birthrights to please the senses for half an hour. The life has no sanctuary, because there is no deity resident within it. It is a lodging place for every vagrant emotion.

I cannot tell the secrets of any human life, and I would not if I could. But review last week—Mastered one hour in the early days by passion that burned on a low level, you answered it. Immediately, some new reason entered into your being and your next action was a response to that appeal. Quickly following upon it some emotion swept over your soul, and you yielded to that, some new purpose dominated you. You are the sport of all the winds that blow. Profane, unholy broods cross and recross the threshold and for the moment possess you. You are like some ancient temple left in ruins—no ministering priest, no resident deity, no ritual, and no worship. But the bats and owls and wandering sons of men cross and recross the threshold! Such is the life of many a man who will do nothing mean in certain directions. Many a man who is far more generous in the makeup of his being than Jacob; many a man—and here is the tragedy of it—who is capable of higher and nobler things than other men can ever climb to; for lack of a central authority, a master principle, recognition of God, is left the sport of all emotions and passions.

Now let us take the story as it leads us a little further. So far we have only been thinking of profanity itself. Now mark what this story reveals to us of profanity in its issue. What is the outcome of this kind of life? I shall confine myself to the illustrations afforded in the case of Esau. What did he lose? His birthright, his blessing, and his opportunity of return, for there was no revoking of the issue of his own choice and his own decision even though he sought the revoking of them with tears.

First of all, he lost his birthright. Let it be recognized, as you have doubtless already recognized, that it is very difficult for Westerners to understand this story. We are sometimes inclined to interpret the sale of the birthright in terms of the material, but that is to entirely miss the central value of it. What was the birthright? The right of the firstborn to be the head of the house, to be priest and king within the family, and, finally, to be the trustee for succeeding generations, to hold the sacred responsibility of the continuity of purpose and power within the family. You will remember that upon one occasion Jesus said to those men of the East who listened to Him, "Fill ye up then the measure of your fathers" (Matt. 23:32). That is an eastern word which we Westerners hardly understand. We have certain affections for those who have gone before us; but this continuity of family responsibility, of family privilege, this sense that we enter into the inheritance of a glorious past, that we are responsible to take that inheritance and pass it on to our children, how little we know of all this. The birthright among those Eastern people meant the responsibility of headship, the responsibility and privilege of ruling within the family and of officiating as priest; therefore the sublime and ultimate value of the birthright was that the man who held it was the trustee for future generations, giving line, direction, temper, tone, and dynamic to those who were to follow him. It was all this that Esau counted as nothing.

I am very much afraid, indeed I will declare, that apart from the illumination of the Holy Spirit, that attempted exposition of what this meant will make little appeal to some men, for we are so terribly in actual and volitional sympathy with Esau that we constantly make the same calculations and come to the same decisions. We say, "I shall die I am so hungry, and what value will the birthright be if I die. Give me the food!" Esau took the pottage, one mess of meat, satisfaction of carnal hunger, perfectly legitimate hunger; but he made it the price in bargaining of the birthright possession. A profane man; a sensual appetite took possession of him for half an hour, and he bartered a spiritual inheritance to satisfy it. We are not so far back as we thought we were! We are not away amid Arab myths. We are face-to-face with living men who are doing exactly the same thing for lack of a deity governing the shrine, for lack of God mastering the life. One sudden animal passion possesses the soul—a passion which in itself may not be wrong, and which satisfied in the right direction may be perfectly legitimate. But in some hour of crisis the spiritual inheritance is abandoned for the satisfaction of the animal appetite, and the birthright it lost. The man was profane and passion held him for a moment, in which moment the strange and awful power of volition acted in such a way that his birthright was lost. That is the supreme and fundamental thing. Because that was supreme and fundamental, the writer of the letter to the Hebrews names it rather than the things that follow.

In that hour he lost not the birthright only, but blessing also;

the realization of all the birthright privileges, the possibility of the fulfillment of the divine purpose in his life, of fellowship in operation with God which would have made him a link in the great chain of the divine movement. He dropped out of the divine march, though not out of the divine government. He lost all the privileges accruing as the result of possession of the birthright.

When being profane he was swept away by the passion of an hour and sold his birthright, he lost the opportunity of repentance, though subsequently he sought it with tears. He did not seek repentance in his own life. It was the revoking of his father's blessing that he sought with tears. But there was found no place of repentance in Isaac's action. Isaac dare not go back upon the blessing, for he had found the overruling God compelling him to cooperate even through the fraud practiced upon him. He said to Esau of Jacob, "I . . . have blessed him? yea, and he shall be blessed" (Gen. 27:33). There was no room for repentance; Isaac could not repent. Esau besought him to change his mind and go back upon the blessing pronounced, but there was no place of repentance found in the attitude of Isaac though this man sought it with tears. What a revelation of the harvest of decision, of the appalling power of choice, of how character takes its direction from such a choice, and of how utterly futile is remorse in the presence of the calamity which is the inevitable nemesis of choice made because a man was profane.

What is the teaching of this story for us? Need I make the inquiry? A profane person is one who lacks the sense of God, and the mastery of God, and who therefore is like a veritable temple with the fire absent from the altar, with the presence absent from the holiest. Its doors are wide open so that whosoever next may pass that way may find lodging there and use it to the destruction of the temple itself. A profane person may never use coarse language, may not have been guilty of venal sin, may never yet have descended to vulgarity. What is a profane person? It is that young man of fine physique, genial heart, and lovable disposition who lacks an indweller who governs the life and masters it. It is one who is devoid of a principle that holds all the elements of his nature in true relationship, poise, balance, and strength. It is the man who rejoices in his natural strength and trusts to his native wit, and answers every moving impulse of his splendid life. It is the man who never prays and never trembles. It the person who is never conscious of the measurement of the ages and the touch of the spiritual. It is the one who lives through the days as though each day had enough within itself for him, and as though there were no harvest to be reaped from the sowings of the passing hours! That is a profane person.

There is no gospel in that. But there is preparation for the declaration of the gospel. I address myself now for a moment to the men who say, "That is true." I think in the course of a message such as I am endeavoring to deliver, the congregation becomes strangely sifted and multitudes drop out. In the last few moments I am after the man who in the quiet, inner shrine of his own nature is saying now, "That is exactly true of me." The temple has been injured, and it is not only true that the threshold has been crossed and recrossed by all who have cared to enter; it is also true that in the crossing and recrossing they have injured the temple itself. It may be some man is saying, "I am profane, not merely in that essential sense but in a vulgar sense. What can I do?"

This building is erected and the Christian religion exists for the delivery of a message to that man. I do not know the end of Esau. I know the measurement of him in the New Testament. But there is a wonderful reticence in its dealings with all these men. I know we have been very busy consigning them all to everlasting perdition. Yes, if Esau continued in his profanity to the very end, he was lost! But I cannot tell because the record is silent.

This, however, I do know. If your life has been profane, if it be profane tonight with that early profanity of irresponsibility, before the wounds are deep and the scars wide or the sins vulgar, I have a message for you. Or if your profanity has become the profanity of a ruined temple in your own consciousness, so that you have no door to shut and the window lights are all broken. If the very building itself is trembling to ruin, and you know it by the fevered brow, the palsied hand, and the tottering step, I have a message for you. My friend, you know it. It is the old, old story. It is the story of One who came into this world, the Son of God, and who in the midst of history said such a remarkable thing as this: "The Son of man is come to seek and to save that which was lost" (Luke 19:10). The vulgarized man, the profane person, the man with all the doors open through which conflicting and contradictory emotions pass and hold high carnival within him and ruin him; the Son of Man has come for that man, to seek him and to save him.

Paul was one of His messengers. Paul knew the Lord Christ and gave himself to Him without reserve. There came a day when Paul went into Corinth, the place of temples, and he looked out upon the men of Corinth and saw them as profane. He preached this evangel, and some men in Corinth heard it and believed and yielded to it. Then having passed away from Corinth, Paul wrote back to these men and said, "Ye are the temple of God" (1 Cor. 3:16). In order that they might not understand him to merely mean that the whole Christian church in its corporate nature is the temple of God, he made his statement personal as he said, "Know ye not that your body is the temple of the Holy Ghost" (6:19). As I have already indicated that word *temple* stands in exact and absolute opposition to the word *profane*. I feel my way into this word *sanctuary* to get at its roots and its first significance, and I find that it means "to dwell." The particular word that Paul used in both these passages is one that would not describe the whole temple to the Jew, but the inner shrine, the sanctuary, the holy of holies reserved for the manifested presence of God, and across the threshold of which no man must tread except by express divine command and permission. Paul said to these Corinthian men, "You are a temple." To the individual he said, "Your body is the temple of the Holy Spirit."

That suggests a graphic and immediate contrast. Here is a

man profane. There is a man who is the sanctuary of the Spirit of God. In the one case, all the doors are open and any who pleases may cross the threshold. In the other case, the doors are closed and One indwells and fills with glory, light, and purity the whole life. All the life is gathered about that central Indweller and is mastered and made under His impulse.

Which is it with you? There are no midway conditions. This whole audience tonight, every human being, the preacher, and all the rest, is divided in the economy of God into two camps. We are profane, or we are sanctuaries of the Spirit. Which? That is a question which no man can answer for his brother, and a question which no man is called upon to answer to his brother. But the answer is already given to the One who alone can read the secret thought and intent of the heart. Which are you?

Here is Jacob—mean, contemptible, dastardly in many ways. Nevertheless, underneath all the meanness of his makeup there is a profound belief in God. In spite of all the foolhardiness of his attempts to help God toward the consummation, at last faith conquers, and because he believes in Him, God is able to take hold of Jacob and make him Israel. Esau, a finer man on the level of the purely human—more genial, more generous, more splendid—but profane; never a single word of him in all the story which suggests his consciousness of God. Easu, the temple doors open, destructive passions lodging for a moment working havoc and passing out only to make way for others, is left to the ruin of the fugitive forces that destroy.

Where are you? The service of the Sabbath will soon be over. I pray you in this evening hour, define your own position. On the heights, in the light of eternity, by the standards and measurements of God, which are you? A temple of the Spirit—not yet a perfected one, the Spirit has much to do before the temple can grow into all loveliness and perfection—but a temple with the Spirit indwelling? Or profane, with the doors all open?

If profane, then remember how the letter to the Corinthians begins, "Unto the church of God which is at Corinth, to them that are sanctified in Christ Jesus" (1 Cor. 1:2). That is the profane made holy, the ruined temple taken possession of. That is the gospel in this evening hour. Even though you are profane, even though the folly of your profanity has already moved to your ruin, He will enter, take possession, and begin the work of restoration. Once undertaken He will never abandon this work until He makes you a habitation of God through the Spirit in all beauty and glory, according to the will of God. May it be ours to yield ourselves to Him and find the Indweller who will work His good, perfect, and acceptable will within us, to the fulfillment of our lives and the glory of God.

Hobab: The Slave of the Second Best

Clovis Gillham Chappell (1882–1972) was one of American Methodism's best-known and most effective preachers. He pastored churches in Washington, D.C.; Dallas and Houston, Texas; Memphis, Tennessee; and Birmingham, Alabama; and his pulpit ministry drew great crowds. He was especially known for his biographical sermons that made biblical figures live and speak to our modern day. He published about thirty volumes of sermons.

This message was taken from *Familiar Failures,* published in 1928 by Doubleday, Doran, and Company, New York.

9

Hobab: The Slave of the Second Best

> We are journeying unto the place of which the LORD said,
> I will give it you: come thou with us, and we will do thee good:
> for the LORD hath spoken good concerning Israel. And he said
> unto him, I will not go; but I will depart to mine own land, and to
> my kindred. And he said, Leave us not, I pray thee; forasmuch as
> thou knowest how we are to encamp in the wilderness, and thou
> mayest be to us instead of eyes. (Numbers 10:29–31)

IT IS USUALLY ASSUMED that Hobab gave heed to Moses and joined with him in his great enterprise. But I do not so read the story. To the first invitation, it stands written in the record that he gave a flat refusal. Then Moses made a second and more pressing appeal. What Hobab said to this, we do not know. The story gives us no hint of his answer. But we never hear of his being with Moses at a later day. For this reason, and also because he has just said, "I will not," it is my personal opinion that he persisted in his original refusal.

No Lack of Opportunity

But if Hobab failed to have a part in this great enterprise, it was not for lack of an opportunity.

He was invited. He seems to have treated the invitation with indifference. If so, his indifference was not born because of the indifference of his friend and kinsman. That is the secret of much of the indifference that we witness today. The reason our children care so little for the things that matter most is often because we care so little. The reason your husband is so little concerned about his personal relationship to Jesus Christ may be because you are so little concerned. The reason your wife gives the church the second or third place in her interests is because that is your attitude. The reason the world finds it so easy to ignore us is often because we are so indifferent to the needs of the world. Moses was interested enough in Hobab to invite him.

Not only did Moses invite Hobab, but he gave the invitation in a most telling way.

Moses invited Hobab personally. I believe in invitations from the pulpit. I believe in the invitation of the Sunday school teacher to the class as a whole. But the most compelling invitation is that which is given personally. The men that Jesus gathered about Him were almost all of them won one by one. I believe in every form of evangelism that induces men to become followers of Christ, but the most effective yet discovered is that of a personal appeal.

He invited him with convincing sincerity. Moses was himself engaged in the enterprise in which he was trying to enlist the interest of his friend. He was investing all that he was and all that he had in this great undertaking. Therefore, there was naturally a strong appeal in his invitation to Hobab. Such invitations always carry weight. But there is little use for me to ask you to do what I myself am unwilling to do. There is little use lecturing your child upon the value of Sunday school when you do not attend it. There is little use preaching to your boy about the worth of the church, when you yourself ignore it. The measure of our power to win others to Christ is the measure of the fullness with which we ourselves are possessed by Him.

Then this invitation was given earnestly. I do not believe that anybody is ever won by the halfhearted. It is the earnest man that grips us. It is the heart on fire that kindles a flame within our own hearts. There is something fascinating about an earnest man. There is something almost irresistible. But how easy it is to resist the lukewarm and the cold and the morally flabby. One earnest man like Peter, with all his lack of training, is worth any dozen men of the Nicodemus type who seem to be too cultured to be enthusiastic.

A few years ago there was a mission worker striving to reach the lost in one of the slums of Chicago. He became interested in an outcast girl. He literally fought with her for her soul. At last he succeeded in winning her. In the joy of her newfound Lord she went back to the home of her childhood. Now it so happened that her father was a man of great wealth. In token of his deep appreciation of the service of this missionary, he made him a present of a vast sum of money amounting to several millions of dollars. I wonder how much it would increase our enthusiasm if we knew that in the winning of one soul we should also win a fortune?

Finally, this invitation was given intelligently. The appeal Moses made to Hobab was a full-orbed appeal. He compelled his brother-in-law to see some of the advantages that would come should he choose to join with him in his great enterprise. He held out inducements that were very alluring. But they were not half so alluring as those that the church of Jesus Christ has to offer today. Moses had that to say which should have appealed strongly to his brother-in-law. We, as members of the church, have an appeal that should be irresistible.

An Irresistible Appeal

What is that appeal?

To follow the lead of Moses, it is the appeal of a promised good. "Come thou with us," said Moses, "and we will do thee good." I dare take this same wooing word upon my lips. I can do so with confidence. I have far more to offer than had this man of the long ago. "Come thou with us." Accept our Lord, enter into our fellowship, and "we will do thee good."

Now, I am perfectly aware that this form of invitation is a bit out of fashion. There are those who tell us that men are no longer appealed to by a promised good. They impress us with the fact that they who seek to win people to Christ by an offer of reward appeal to low and selfish motives. But whether such appeal is right or wrong, I can say with certainty that the Bible is not above making it. This it does, not once, but over and over again.

"Ho, every one that thirsteth, come ye to the waters, and he that hath no money; come ye, buy, and eat; yea, come, buy wine and milk without money and without price" (Isa. 55:1). Such was the appeal made by an inspired prophet of long ago. He offered drink to the thirsty and food to the hungry, if they would only come. And the Master Himself is not above making an appeal of the same nature: "If any man thirst, let him come unto me, and drink" (John 7:37). Again He gave this winsome invitation to the tired and the burdened: "Come unto me, all ye that labour and are heavy laden, and I will give you rest" (Matt. 11:28). Over and over again does God hold out to those whom He seeks to win the offer of a sure reward.

What have we as members of the church of Jesus Christ to offer men today?

We offer you a satisfying Savior. We offer you a Master who will meet your deepest needs. "What has Christianity that we do not possess?" asked an Indian scholar of Stanley Jones. "Christ," was the prompt answer. "We have Christ." Of course the Indian intended to argue about the relative merits of ethical codes. But to this answer he had no adequate reply. He knew that he had nothing to offer that could possibly compare with Jesus Christ.

Did you come into this place heart hungry? We offer you the Bread of Life. Are you parched with thirst? Has a moral drought got you in its torturing grip? We offer you the Water of Life. Has sin taken you in its foul fingers and tarnished you and made you unclean? We offer you One who is able to save to the uttermost. He can so wash you that you shall be whiter than snow. He can give you the peace that passes all understanding. He can satisfy your longing soul. He can send you away singing:

> Thou, Oh Christ, art all I want;
> More than all, in Thee I find.

We offer you a worthy goal. "We are journeying unto a place," said Moses to the man whom he sought to win. We also are on our way to a land of promise. The land we seek is not simply the heavenly home up yonder. We are seeking to make a heavenly place out of this present world. We are on our way to a land flowing with the milk of human kindness and sweetened with the honey of brotherhood. We are struggling toward that land where the will of God shall be done on earth as it is done in heaven. Our goal is the complete triumph of Jesus Christ.

We offer you also the privilege of progress. "We are journeying," said Moses. So are we. We have not yet arrived, but we are on our way. We have not attained the heights, but our faces are set in that direction. "We are journeying." I like the word. I love the thought of progress. How dull it is to do "the goose step" like a bunch of raw recruits. There is no fun in standing still. There is no thrill in slipping back. But to journey, to glimpse new scenery, to climb new mountain heights, that is worthwhile.

And that good we can offer you. If you walk with Him, you will be privileged to experience the joy of continuous progress. You will have the fascination of new discoveries. Prosaic monotony will give place to winsome poetry. Every day will bring you a gladsome adventure into a new country. You will make progress until you reach the end of the earthly journey. Then your progress will not be stayed, but quickened. You will go on climbing one Alpine height after another in the land of eternal progress. For "it doth not yet appear what we shall be: but we know that, when he shall appear, we shall be like him; for we shall see him as he is" (1 John 3:2).

A final good we offer you is that of a helpful and bracing fellowship. "Come thou with us," said Moses, "and we will do thee good." "But you have quite a peevish and cantankerous crowd," Hobab might have answered. That would have been quite true. But with all their faults, they were the hope of the world. With all of their faults, the world could have spared any dozen nations better than it could have spared them. "Yes, they are faulty enough," Moses might have said, "but they will make history one day. Besides, I would like to introduce you to two young men, Caleb and Joshua, who are already well worth knowing."

"Come thou with us." I dare make that as my appeal. "But the church is very faulty," you say. I grant it. If we were perfect, you would feel exceedingly uncomfortable among us. In fact, you could not endure our fellowship. Besides, with all our faults, the world is getting its best chance at our hands. We are not the ones, as a rule, that are trampling underfoot the integrities that hold civilization together. We are the ones that, above all others, are trying to preach and trying to live that righteousness that exalted a nation. Therefore, I am not ashamed to say, "Come thou with us, and we will do thee good."

The second appeal that Moses made to Hobab was the privilege of being of service. "Leave us not, I pray thee; forasmuch as thou knowest how we are to encamp in the wilderness and thou mayest be to us instead of eyes." If you do not care for the good that we have to offer you, then we care for the good that you may do us. We are in need. You have it in your power to help that need. Come, therefore, and help us.

Now, if there are those who object to the former appeal, nobody can object to this latter. I am ready to confess that in some measure we are in the wilderness. This is true of the whole world. There is hate between nation and nation. We are still preparing for war. Lawlessness everywhere stalks abroad. This is in part true of the church. It is also true of countless individuals. Broken hearts are all about us. Many have lost their faith and have been swept from their moorings. Everywhere there is need. We are a needy church. We are a needy world.

What is going to be your attitude toward this need? You are

not going to cure it by letting it alone. If the church is not what it ought to be, you are not going to help it by standing aloof from it. You are not going to help by leaving your membership a thousand miles away. You are not going to help by criticizing or throwing stones. If we are not what we ought to be, if we are not doing what we ought to do, then come and help us to do better.

Hobab was to be to them instead of eyes. What a fine vocation! To help folks to see in any realm is magnificent. I remember a teacher of English who was skilled in the fine art of being eyes to his pupils. Prose seemed to become poetry at his touch, and poetry came to be possessed of a more winsome and fascinating music. That is the privilege of the poet. Before the coming of Sidney Lanier what an unsightly spot was the marshes of Glynn! It wearied us with its monotony. It offended us with its croaking. But Sidney Lanier made us to see it as it was. When we saw it, it ceased to croak and began to sing. It became vocal with the love of God.

> As the marsh hen secretly builds on the watery sod,
> Behold, I will build me a nest on the greatness of God!
> I will fly in the greatness of God as the marsh hen flies
> In the freedom that fills all the space 'twixt the marsh and
>   the skies:
> By so many roots as the marsh grass sends in the sod,
> Behold, I will heartily lay me ahold on the greatness of God!
> Oh, like to the greatness of God is the greatness within
> The range of the marshes, the liberal marshes of Glynn.

"Thou mayest be to us instead of eyes." To help people to see new beauties in goodness, new beauties in truth, new beauties in holiness, how supremely worthwhile! We may help them to see even Jesus Christ Himself! Stanley tells us that when he left for Africa he was an atheist. But he came home a Christian. This he did because he had seen Christ in David Livingstone. Livingstone had been to him instead of eyes.

The Response

What response did Hobab make to this winsome invitation?

He did not become angry at Moses and tell him to mind his own business. He did not set himself to the task of organizing an army to fight against him and his people. He was not antagonistic in the least. It is highly probable that he wished Moses well in his great undertaking. But this seems to have been his answer—"I will depart to mine own land and to my kindred."

Now the pathos of his choice was not that he decided upon a base and shameful course. It was rather in the fact that, by his refusal to accept this invitation, he chose the second best when he might have had the best. There is no indication that through this wrong decision he went to the lowest depths. He only failed to reach the fine heights that were within his reach. And my fear for you who turn a deaf ear to the appeal of Christ is not that any great number of you will become rakes or crooks. But it is this rather—that you will become so absorbed in the second best that you will miss the best.

A few years ago a mother who lived near my old home was doing her week's washing. She was out by the well some distance from the house. Upon looking up from her task, she saw that her house was in flames. She dashed into the burning building and brought out a few quilts. Then back she went and brought out a featherbed and one or two pillows. Then the house reeled and staggered like a drunken man and fell in ruins. But the screams of this mother sounded above the crash of the building and the roar of the flames. She was remembering too late that she had left her baby asleep in that house.

Now the tragedy of this mother's blunder was not in the fact that she had saved a featherbed and a pillow or two. There was no harm in that. It was not that she had saved a few quilts. There is not the least harm in saving quilts. The tragedy was that she became so absorbed in the things of secondary value that she forgot that which was of supreme value. That danger, in one form or another, threatens every one of us. Hence, I call you to the choice of the highest, even Jesus Christ, our Lord.

NOTES

Judas (Not Iscariot)

John Daniel Jones (1865–1942) served for forty years at the Richmond Hill Congregational Church in Bournemouth, England, where he ministered the Word with a remarkable consistency of quality and effectiveness, as his many volumes of published sermons attest. A leader in his denomination, he gave himself to church extension (he helped to start thirty new churches), assistance to needier congregations, and increased salaries for the clergy. He spoke at D. L. Moody's Northfield Conference in 1919.

This sermon was taken from his book *Richmond Hill Sermons,* published in 1932 by Hodder and Stoughton, London.

JOHN DANIEL JONES

10

Judas (Not Iscariot)

Judas (not Iscariot). (John 14:22 ASV)

"Not many wise . . . not many noble, are called," said Paul about the membership of the early Christian church. The membership of that church was composed of the weak things, the base things, and the despised things of the world. It was a collection of people, who, from the worldly point of view, were mere "nobodies."

What Paul says about the church may be said, with equal truth, about the apostolate—that group of twelve men whom Jesus chose out of the whole multitude of disciples that they might be with Him, and that He might send them forth to preach—the twelve men who constitute the foundation of the Christian church. They, too, from the point of view of worldly station, were a collection of "nobodies." The only exception to that statement may have been Judas Iscariot. He was the only one of the Twelve who was not a Galilean, and the fact that he was made treasurer of the little groups seems to suggest that he was a man of some substance. But of the other eleven, four at least, and probably six, were fishermen. One was an ex-tax collector. One was a Jewish Sinn Feiner. Of the rest, we know nothing at all.

But though they were "nobodies" from the worldly point of view, we know that there were among the Twelve three or four men of quite conspicuous gift. Gift is not a matter of rank or even of education. Among men who earn their bread by the sweat of their brows, and who have had none of the advantages of a university education, may be discovered men of forceful personality and great spiritual gift. And so among these twelve we find Peter, who was a born leader; John, who was a man of supreme spiritual genius; James, who was a man of fiery zeal and of great force of personality (I gather that from the fact that he was the first of the apostles to be seized and martyred. Herod struck at James because he was one of the most aggressive leaders of the new sect.); and Matthew, who wielded the pen of a ready writer. But of the rest it must be said that they were just plain ordinary men, with no conspicuous gift at all. They are in the background of the apostolic group. We know a little about Andrew and Philip and Thomas. But there are four others who figure in practically no incident. They did nothing in particular. There they are—James the son of Alphaeus, Bartholomew, Simon (who was called the Zealot), and Judas the son of James—mere names and nothing more, men about whom we know practically nothing at all.

Somebody has asked why it was that Jesus chose humble men of this kind to be his first apostles. Dr. A. B. Bruce's answer to that question is that Jesus had to be content with the best He could get—and I daresay the answer is the right one. Jesus did not have the whole nation to select from. When our government wants a committee or a commission to inquire into some problem, it can call upon the services of the very best men, and the best men think it an honor and a privilege to serve. But Jesus wasn't in that position. None of the rulers or Pharisees believed in Him. Perhaps He would have liked to have had men like Nicodemus and Joseph of Arimathea among His apostles. But they didn't give Him the chance of calling them, for they were too timid to openly confess Him. Jesus had to take what He could get—He was compelled to choose His apostles from among those humble folk who listened to His gospel.

But while the prosaic matter-of-fact reason may have been that Jesus had to take what He could get, I like to think that there was divine wisdom in the choice. Paul says that one reason why God chose the weak things, the base things, and the despised things of the world was that it might be clear to everybody that the excellence of the power was of God. For these weak things, base things, and despised things of the world turned the world upside down. They overthrew things that were mighty and brought to nothing the things that were. Nobody could believe that the power that accomplished such amazing things resided in the early Christians themselves—people were compelled to believe that the divine power was working in and through them.

And all that holds good of the apostles. Had they been a group of geniuses—had one of them been a Socrates in his dialectic skill, another a Plato in his soaring vision, and another a Demosthenes or a Cicero in his eloquence—people might have said that their triumphs were due to their own genius. But they couldn't say it, seeing that (as the Sanhedrin said of Peter and John) they were unlearned and ignorant men. With a kind of awe men felt that the divine power was working in and through them.

And then I like to think that it was not simply because He couldn't get anyone else that Jesus chose fishermen and suchlike humble folk for His first apostles. I like to think that the character of the religion Jesus came to preach was symbolized in the character of His apostolate. Other religions were largely exclusive. The Eleusinian mysteries were only for the initiated. Plato's philosophy was only for the select few. The Judaism of our Lord's day ruled out all publicans and sinners. But Jesus had room in His heart for the humblest and the poorest. You remember how again and again the New Testament emphasizes the fact that His gospel was to be good news to the poor. A poor village maiden was chosen to be the Messiah's mother.

Mary, in that one fact, saw proof of God's regard for the humble and poor of the earth. "He hath put down princes from their thrones," she sang, "And hath exalted them of low degree" (Luke 1:52). "The Spirit of the Lord is upon me," said Jesus, in the first sermon He preached at Nazareth, "because he anointed me to preach good tidings to the poor" (4:18). To the poor! To earth's despised and neglected folk, to those for whom Plato and the Pharisees had no use. His was a gospel for everybody—for the toiling millions as well as for the cultured few. That blessed truth was symbolized in the fact that it was fishermen and suchlike plain, hardworking, humble folk He chose for His first apostles.

But even of these apostles—as I have already hinted—there were some less gifted and conspicuous than others. Peter, John, James, Matthew and—in a lesser degree, Andrew and Thomas—played a fairly prominent part in the course of Christ's ministry and the subsequent history of the early church. But the rest of them were not principal actors. They remain in the background, in the shadows. And yet I read that on the foundation stones of the Eternal City there are graven the names of the Twelve Apostles of the Lamb. It is not the names of Peter, John, Matthew, and Thomas alone that are there, but the names of these men of whom nothing is recorded—James the son of Alphaeus, Bartholomew, Simon (who was called the Zealot), and Judas the son of James—are there too. They did their bit. They used their talent. They were not gifted or brilliant perhaps, but they were faithful men and so their names stand side by side with the names of Peter and John.

From all of which I deduce a couple of plain and yet heartening lessons. A great deal of the world's work is done by plain and humble men who never come into the limelight and get little by way of earthly recognition. We concentrate attention on the captain and the officers, in their gold lace, on the bridge. But below, unseen of the passengers, are the stokers and the engineers without whom the ship could not sail a mile. We concentrate our attention upon the political heads of our state departments. They are the people who are in the limelight. But behind them stand the men and women of the permanent Civil service, who really do the work. We concentrate our attention upon the architect who designs a new monument or a new bridge. But the architect would be helpless without the carpenter, the bricklayer, the stonemason, the iron founder, and the riveter. At a concert, when an orchestra has given an inspired rendering of some musical masterpiece, the audience in its enthusiasm cheers the conductor, but I have seen a conductor, after bowing his own thanks, wave his hand to his orchestra and bid them rise—as if to say to the audience, "These are the people to whom the thanks are due. Without them I could have done nothing."

And it is like that in the realm of religion. The real work of the church is being done by a great host of quiet, humble folk who labor away unnoticed and unapplauded of men. The Peters and Johns of the church are few. It is good, of course, to have the great preachers who can arouse and inspire great congregations, who can go about and preach eloquent sermons at special services. But although the religious press concentrates upon them and everybody talks about them, they are not the people who do the work of the church. The real work of the church is being done by quiet ministries carried on in towns and villages by faithful ministers, who do their bit of work unknown to fame—Sunday school teachers, members of choirs, devoted men and women who are assiduous in prayer, those who visit the sick and comfort the sad and minister to the needy. No trumpet calls attention to their labor. The newspapers never proclaim their names, but these Jameses and Simons and Bartholomews and Judases—the "bravely dumb who do their deed and scorn to blot it with a name"—these are the people who do the real work of Christ's church.

And the second lesson I gather is this—that the unnoticed labor of earth is noticed and recorded in heaven. No chronicler has set down anything to the credit of James the son of Alphaeus, Bartholomew, Simon, or Judas the son of James.

There was nothing shining or outstanding about their ministries. They were men of two talents. But they used those talents faithfully, and God did not overlook their work of faith and labor of love. Their names are to be found alongside of those of Peter, James, and John on the foundations of the Eternal City. God does not forget. God does not overlook. The cup of cold water given in the name of a disciple by no means loses its reward. A day will come when the humblest toiler in the most obscure field will hear the Master say, "Good and faithful servant" (Matt. 25:21, 23), and will discover that God was watching him all the time. And that is what matters—not to have our names in the newspapers, but to have them in the Lamb's Book of Life.

> Men heed thee, love thee, praise thee not.
> The Master praises; What are men?

But you may well ask me, "What about Judas, not Iscariot, all this time?" And I must confess I had not meant to have said all this about those unknown disciples of whom he was one. But now let me concentrate upon Judas.

And the first thing I want you to notice about him is this—that he seems to have had a variety of names. There are, as you know, in the New Testament four lists of the apostles. In Matthew's list there is no mention of a second Judas, but there is a disciple called Thaddaeus who is named in close connection with James the son of Alphaeus. Mark agrees with Matthew in naming Thaddaeus and not Judas. In Luke's account, however, we find no Thaddaeus, but (both in the gospel and in the book of Acts) we have Judas the son of James. Now, the great probability is that Thaddaeus and Judas the son of James are one and the same person. That there was a second Judas in the apostolate we know, of course, from this phrase of my text where he is differentiated from Iscariot. Now, when we look a little bit more closely at the verses, two or three rather interesting things emerge. The first is this, there was one case of a father and son being both members of the apostolate. The Authorized Version translates Judas the *brother* of James. But that will never do. The Greek simply will not bear it. Judas was not James's brother; he was James's son. There was more than one pair of *brothers* in the apostolate. Peter and Andrew were brothers; James and John were brothers; possibly Thomas and Matthew were brothers. But the only case of father and son was James the son of Alphaeus and Judas the son of James. It is considered rather a noteworthy thing when father and son both sit together in Parliament. It is a still more noteworthy thing that father and son should be together in the small circle of our Lord's chosen friends. I can imagine that James's heart was warmed when his son enlisted in the same service as he, and I can imagine that James's crowning joy came when Jesus invited his son as well as him to be an apostle.

But what about this other name, Thaddaeus? My own feeling is that it was Jesus' pet name for him. He wasn't the only one to whom He gave a new name. He called Simon *Peter*. I think He gave Levi the new name of Matthew, so I believe He gave Judas the son of James this new name of Thaddaeus. And He didn't give it to him to distinguish him from the Iscariot. He gave it to him because it answered to Judas's character. The names we give to people at baptism are, in the nature of things, mere labels. They cannot be an index to character, for character is not then formed. Every John is not the grace of God, every Theodore is not the gift of God, and every Catherine is not pure. If we waited until we all grew up and character had revealed itself, names might be made to correspond to character. Now what Jesus did was to give Judas a name that suggested his character. He called him Thaddaeus, and that word Thaddaeus means "cheery," "courageous," "lively." One of the commentators suggests that he was a Mark Tapley kind of person—courageously optimistic, a sort of foil to the melancholy Thomas. And I daresay the happy, cheery, optimistic spirit of Judas was often a comfort to Jesus. The very name speaks of our Lord's appreciation of him. He was a bright, cheery, courageous soul.

But I still haven't touched upon the special point that drew my attention to this phrase. Matthew and Mark drop the name Judas altogether. The other Judas had made it unsavory. Luke and John retain his original name Judas, but Luke takes care to distinguish him as the "son of James," and, in the phrase of my text, John specifically differentiates him from the other Judas—"Judas *not* Iscariot." It is as if John said, "I don't want you to mix up this Judas with the traitor. He bears the same name—but this is Judas *not* Iscariot."

And the first simple and elementary lesson I gather from this phrase is that of the need to *discriminate*. We are much given to passing general judgments, and our general judgments are nearly always wrong. We pass general judgments, for example, upon nations and peoples. We have a sort of general notion of the American. "Uncle Sam" stands in the public mind as a rather uncouth and flamboyant person, mainly concerned with the almighty dollar. Well everyone who knows anything about America knows how silly such a general judgment is—there are as gracious, cultivated Christian folk in America as there are in this England of ours. The general conception of the Scotsman is that he is a very closefisted kind of person, a man who looks at a shilling half a dozen times before he parts with it. And yet those of us who know anything at all about the work of pleading for charities, know that among the most generous and openhanded of our givers are people who hail from north of the Tweed. My own countrymen labor under the imputation that they are not specially truthful. It is an imputation that we have every right to resent. No doubt there are untruthful folks in Wales, but then they are not altogether unknown in this England. On the other hand there are among the Welsh people of as nice and scrupulous a sense of honor as any you will find in England.

Sweeping judgments are always wrong, and if we do not want to be guilty of injustice we had better learn to discriminate. "You can't indict a nation," said Burke, "and you can't indict a class." You remember the sweeping judgment Tennyson's northern farmer pronounces on the poor: "The poor in the lump," he said, "are bad." And yet when we stay to think, we know that the virtues of kindness, honesty, helpfulness, self-sacrifice, and real godliness are to be found among the poor as frequently as among any other social class. It would go far to soften asperities if we refrained from uncompromising judgments and learned to discriminate. We have our political parties in this country, and we differ in our views of what is really for the good of our country. And to listen to the way we sometimes talk, one might imagine that all the people in the other parties were knaves and humbugs and traitors. It will be all to the good when we realize that the people who differ from us may be just as sincere and wholehearted in their love of country as we are ourselves. If we want to judge fairly we must avoid sweeping generalizations and learn to discriminate.

And the second truth this little phrase suggested to me (and it was the truth on which I had meant to lay the chief emphasis) was this: how a bad man can bring *dishonor upon a name.* Judas Iscariot by his treachery had made the very name Judas a name of shame and disgrace. I have noticed, sometimes, advertisements in our newspapers in which the advertiser begs the public to take notice that he is not to be identified with, and has no connection with, some other person who may have been brought up in the courts for some offense against the law. If a man, for example, has been convicted of fraud, it makes it difficult for another business man who may happen to bear the same name. So he has to put a notice in the papers. "It is true my name is so and so, but I am not the so and so convicted in the courts the other day." Judas—not Iscariot! One bad man can bring disgrace upon a name! One of the meekest, saintliest men I ever knew bore the name of Crippen, but somehow his name always used to call to mind another Crippen, a notorious and wicked murderer. He had made the very name Crippen hateful in the ears of honest and peaceful men. The name Englishman is an honorable name, but a bad man can make it a name of scorn. What the primitive peoples, to whom our people travel in search of adventure or trade, think of the name "Englishman" depends on how our representatives behave when they get among them. A bad Englishman—a man who exploits the natives and oppresses them, a man who sees in them opportunities for the gratification of his greed and his lust—will make the very name to stink in the nostrils of those who suffer at his hands. What do you suppose the natives of Africa must have thought of Englishmen in the eighteenth century when they were foremost in the conduct of the slave trade with all its horrors? And what must they think of England still when they judge our race from certain traders of evil life who see in the helplessness of the natives simply an opportunity to get rich quickly? A bad man makes the name he bears hateful while a good man like Livingstone, or our own Stanley Worth, makes the very name fragrant and honored.

And it is like that with the name Christian, which is the practical point to which I want to lead up the whole of this discussion. A bad Christian can make the very name a name of contempt—just as Iscariot by his treachery cast an indelible stigma upon the very name Judas. People judge Christianity by Christians. They judge our faith by the people who profess it. We may think that unfair. We may contend, and with a certain justice, that Christianity ought to be judged by Christ, or at least by the standards set forth in the New Testament, and not by any inadequate attempts made by Christians to live up to these standards. But it is of little use our objecting. It is by the lives of Christians men will judge Christianity. They will judge the tree by its fruits. And a bad Christian can bring the whole Christian name into contempt. And isn't that why Christianity is at such a discount in our world just now? Isn't that why we are so ineffective and unimpressive? We are such poor Christians! A selfish Christian, an unkind Christian, a Christian who is just as keen as anyone else upon worldly goods, a Christian who gets money unjustly—he simply brings the whole of the Christian religion into contempt.

Dr. Hutton told a story in the *British Weekly* not long ago—a terrible story—about a theatrical performance in Paris in the course of the Dreyfus affair. In the production the church had played an ignoble part. In the course of the performance a voice said, "Down with the church," and the whole audience echoed it. And then another voice more daring cried, "Down with Jesus," but that cry was heard in silence. But what a condemnation of the church which is supposed to teach and body forth the Christian religion! Down with the church! Men are not shouting that out loud today. They are just leaving the church and neglecting the religion it represents. Christians by their poor living have made the world feel there is nothing much in the Christian faith. Well, what sort of Christians are we? Are we by our lives recommending or discrediting the Christian faith? What men will see in Jesus and our Christian religion depends upon what they see in us. "Either put on courage," said Alexander to a soldier who was shirking the battle, "or put off the name of Alexander." Cowardice was shameful in a soldier. And selfishness and hardness and unkindness are shameful in a Christian. It is a terrifying thought to me that by unworthy living we may make the name Christian a name of scorn and contempt. That we may be saved from that reproach, we ought to make that old couplet our prayer:

> So let our lips and lives express,
> The holy gospel we profess.
> So let our works and virtues shine,
> To prove the doctrine all divine.

Onesiphorus: A Friend in Chains

Clarence Edward Noble Macartney (1879–1957) ministered in Paterson, New Jersey, and Philadelphia, Pennsylvania, before assuming the influential pastorate of First Presbyterian Church, Pittsburgh, Pennsylvania, where he ministered for twenty-seven years. His preaching especially attracted men, not only to the Sunday services but also to his popular Tuesday noon luncheons. He was gifted in dealing with Bible biographies and, in this respect, has been called "the American Alexander Whyte." Much of his preaching was topical-textual, but it was always biblical, doctrinal, and practical. Perhaps his most famous sermon is "Come Before Winter."

The sermon I have selected was taken from *The Woman of Tekoah*, published in 1955 by Pierce and Washabaugh.

CLARENCE EDWARD NOBLE MACARTNEY

11

Onesiphorus: A Friend in Chains

And was not ashamed of my chain. (2 Timothy 1:16)

THERE WERE SOME OF Paul's friends who were ashamed of his chain. In the day of danger and adversity they forsook him. But not this faithful friend from Ephesus.

Chains are the test of friendship. They show whether it is just a fair-weather friendship or a friendship born for adversity. Those who wrote the ancient fables were great preachers. One of the famous fables was that of the two travelers and the bear. On their journey the travelers suddenly encountered a bear. One in great fear immediately climbed into a tree and hid himself without a thought of his companion. The other, with no chance to go anywhere and having heard that a bear will not touch a dead body, threw himself on the ground and pretended to be dead. The bear came up and began to nuzzle him and sniff at his nose and mouth and ears, and, thinking him dead, went off.

When the bear was out of sight, the one who had climbed the tree came down and asked his friend what it was that the bear had whispered to him. "For," he said, "I noticed that he put his mouth very close to your ear." The other said, "It was no great secret that he told me. What he said was to have a care how I kept company with those who, when trouble or danger arises, desert their friends and leave them in the lurch."

The old fables strike true and ever-resounding chords of human experience and relationship. Never more so than this fable of the two travelers and the bear. Paul had many warm friends. Let no one think of the apostle as pure and cold intellect. He did indeed have a great mind, but his heart was still greater. Chrysostom, the golden-mouthed preacher of Antioch, in what is perhaps the greatest tribute ever written of Paul, at the end of his sermons on the letter to the Romans, says that of all the cities of the world he loves Rome most. He loves it most not because of the great Caesars that reigned there, but because Paul died there. There he could see "the dust of that heart which a man would not do wrong to call the heart of the world; so enlarged that it could take in cities and nations and peoples; a heart which burned at each one that was lost; which despised both death and hell; and yet was broken down by a brother's tears."

Paul's Friends

Among the friends of Paul whom he names and salutes in his letters was Mark, who had failed in his first relationship with Paul. Because he had deserted him and turned back at Perga on the first missionary journey, Paul would not permit Mark to accompany him on the second journey. Afterward, given a second chance, Mark "made good." At the very end of his life, Paul, in his last letter to Timothy, asks him to bring Mark with him "for he is profitable to me for the ministry" (2 Tim. 4:11).

Others of Paul's friends were Silas, who went with him on the second journey; Onesimus, the fugitive slave of Philemon converted by Paul at Rome; Epaphroditus, the friend from the church at Philippi who came to see Paul when he was a prisoner at Rome; Priscilla and Aquila, who risked their lives to help him; Titus, who brought him comforting news about the church at Corinth; Tychicus, the "beloved brother" (Eph. 6:21; Col. 4:7), who carried Paul's letters to the Ephesians and the

Colossians; Tertius, his amanuensis, who took down by dictation the letter to the Romans; Amplias, "beloved in the Lord" (Rom. 16:8); Timothy, "my beloved son" (1 Cor. 4:17) and the friend whom Paul at the very end wanted to come to him at Rome—"come before winter" (2 Tim. 4:21); and last, but not least, Luke, the "beloved physician" (Col. 4:14), whom Paul hands down to immortality with that imperishable encomium, "Only Luke is with me" (2 Tim. 4:11). What a list of friends were on Paul's prayer calendar, and he on theirs!

Not all of Paul's friends, however, were faithful. Before we come to this beautiful mention of Onesiphorus, Paul writes, "This thou knowest, that all they which are in Asia be turned away from me; of whom are Phygellus and Hermogenes" (2 Tim. 1:15). That is all we know of these two friends, who, together with others from the province of Asia, forsook Paul when he was in trouble and in prison. Another friend who was not faithful to the end was Demas, perhaps from the church at Thessalonica, of whom Paul writes, "Demas hath forsaken me, having loved this present world" (4:10). In two earlier letters Paul had sent the salutations of Demas with his own to the disciples at Colosse and Philippi.

In contrast with these friends who forsook him in his hour of need, Paul writes this beautiful word about Onesiphorus, the friend from Ephesus, who came to see him when he was in prison at Rome:

> The Lord give mercy unto the house of Onesiphorus; for he oft refreshed me, and was not ashamed of my chain: But, when he was in Rome, he sought me out very diligently, and found me. The Lord grant unto him that he may find mercy of the Lord in that day: and in how many things he ministered unto me at Ephesus, thou knowest very well. (1:16–18)

Prayers for the Dead

Before we go further in this story of a friend who was not afraid or ashamed of chains, we mention in passing that these words about Onesiphorus, perhaps the only ones in the Bible, are frequently appealed to as scriptural warrant for prayers for the dead. It is pointed out that Paul asks mercy for the *house*—that is, the family—of Onesiphorus. When he does ask mercy to Onesiphorus, it is that he may "find mercy of the Lord in that day" (v. 18)—that is, the day of judgment.

We cannot be certain from the reading of Paul's reference to Onesiphorus that this Ephesian friend was dead. Perhaps he was with Paul at Rome when the letter was written, and that is why Paul asks the great blessing of God's mercy upon his family. Nor because Paul expresses the pious desire that Onesiphorus may find mercy in the day of judgment does it necessarily follow that he was dead. Long before any controversy arose between Catholics and Protestants over prayers for the dead, ancient church fathers, Thodoret and Chrysostom among them, held the view that Onesiphorus was living when Paul wrote the letter to Timothy.

But whether Onesiphorus was living or dead, all that Paul asks is that his great kindness to him when he was in prison shall not be forgotten in the day of judgment when the books are opened. We can be sure that it will be remembered, for in his great preview of the judgment Jesus said that the King will say to those on his right hand, "I was an hungered, and ye gave me meat: I was thirsty, and ye gave me drink: I was a stranger, and ye took me in: Naked, and ye clothed me: I was sick, and ye visited me: I was in prison, and ye came unto me. . . . Inasmuch as ye have done it unto one of the least of these my brethren, ye have done it unto me" (Matt. 25:35–40). This, after all, is the great thing to remember here, and the great and beautiful thing to imitate, that to show mercy to those in distress is pleasing to God and will not go unremembered.

The logic of the gospel is against prayers for the dead, certainly the elaborated machinery of prayers for the dead that finds expression in masses for the dead. The salvation of the soul rests upon the great work of Christ on the cross for sinners, not upon the prayers of even the most pious and devout.

Jesus said to the dying robber, "Today shalt thou be with me in paradise" (Luke 23:43). What more than that could we ask for, if we did pray for the dead? If they are with Christ in paradise, they need no prayer from us.

But because we do not pray for the dead, nor find in the Bible any ground for doing so, it does not follow that we dismiss the beloved dead from our thought. By no means. If one has for years prayed for a dear child, parent, brother or sister, husband or wife, or friend, will he suddenly cease to think of them or make mention of them before God? Certainly not.

I have loved ones in the King's country, and I frequently mention their names in my prayers. But in this way: I pray that the memory of them, the faith and Christlike spirit which were in them, shall influence my own life and make me like them. Thus it is that the dead live again in lives made better by the thought of them.

Onesiphorus and Paul's Chain

It was dangerous for Christians at Rome to let it be known that they were the friends of Paul the prisoner. As we have seen, many could not meet that test of friendship and fell away from Paul. Not so Onesiphorus. We gather from the narrative that Onesiphorus had difficulty in finding where Paul was imprisoned, for Paul says, "He sought me out very diligently, and found me" (2 Tim. 1:17). Some would not have searched at all; others would have satisfied their conscience with just one effort and then abandoned the quest. But Onesiphorus kept searching until he found Paul. When he found him, he cheered him and refreshed him.

Can you not see Onesiphorus with a basket on his arm, perhaps a newly woven robe, too, going here and there in Rome—to the market place, amid the throng at the Forum, at the Capitoline Hill, and at the palace and the barracks—seeking for Paul, and sometimes roughly and rudely and threateningly repulsed by the guards and the soldiers? Yet the kind, noble, and courageous soul did not give up the search. Perhaps it was days or months before he located Paul in that vast and crowded city. And can you not see him as, having found Paul, he took out of his basket those refreshments and that robe and handed them over to Paul? Then he told him news of Timothy and the church at Ephesus? And all the little kindnesses he showed him, as long as the guards permitted him to visit the jail?

In *Great Expectations,* Charles Dickens tells how the boy Pip went to visit for the last time his benefactor, Magwitch, the dying convict, who had been condemned to be hanged. The convict took Pip's hand and said, "You've never deserted me, dear boy. . . . And what's best of all, you've been more comfortable alonger me since I was under a dark cloud than when the sun shone. That's best of all." Yes, it is not when the sun is shining, but when the clouds gather and darkness comes down and our friend wears a chain that friendship comes to its most beautiful flower.

Sir Philip Sidney, poet, philosopher, and soldier of the sixteenth century, fell in battle on the field of Zutphen in 1586. In his great distress he called for a drink of water. But as he was putting the cup to his lips, he saw near him another dying man whose eyes were fixed longingly on the cup. Lowering his hand, Sidney handed him the cup, saying, "Thy necessity is greater than mine." Acts like that have made his name immortal for kindness and grace. It was not strange, therefore, that a knight of that age asked that this epitaph be put upon his grave: "Here lies the friend of Sir Philip Sidney." If you had asked Onesiphorus what epitaph he desired, I am sure he would have said, "Here lies the friend of Paul." But if you had asked Paul to write the epitaph for Onesiphorus, I am sure it would have been this: "Here lies one who was not ashamed of my chain."

The man who wrote the following lines, whoever he was, wrote on the assumption that Onesiphorus was dead when Paul mentioned him in his letter to Timothy. As we have seen, this is not a necessary assumption. Nevertheless, these lines on Onesiphorus bring out for us the beautiful deed of Onesiphorus and how Paul repaid that deed with prayer and gratitude:

> Timotheus, when here and there you go
> Through Ephesus upon your pastoral round,
> Where every street to me is hallowed ground,
> I will be bold and ask you to bestow
> Kindness upon one home, where long ago
> A helpmate lived, whose like is seldom found;
> And when the sweet spring flowers begin to blow,
> Sometime for me, lay one upon his mound.

One of the many shameful things that Jean Jacques Rousseau relates of himself in his celebrated *Confessions* is his reaction when, as he and his companion with whom he had been wandering over France reached Lyons, his friend had an attack of epilepsy on the public square. Rousseau, instead of going to his succor, fled from the scene and abandoned him to the mercy of strangers. He was ashamed of his chain. If to do that is base and ignoble, then to help a friend in chains is the mark of a noble character.

When Martin Luther was entering the bishop's palace at Worms to answer before the emperor and the Diet, and there make his great stand for Christ and for truth, an old knight clapped him on the shoulder and said: "My dear monk, my poor monk, thou art going to make such a stand as neither I nor any of my companions in arms have ever made in our hottest battles. If thou art sure of the justice of thy cause, then forward in God's name, and be of good courage! God will not forsake thee!" He was not ashamed of Luther's chain.

Years ago in Philadelphia a bank failed. There had been dishonesty on the part of some connected with the bank. Among others, a shadow had fallen unjustly over the name of an officer of the bank who was also prominent in church affairs. One morning he received a letter. When he opened it, he saw just one sheet of paper. On the sheet was drawn a man's hand and under the hand the name of one of his friends.

A verse in Proverbs says, "A friend loveth at all times, and a brother is born for adversity" (17:17). Alas, there are many friends, fair-weather friends, who are not born for adversity. Adversity is the wind that separates the chaff of flattery from the grain of real friendship. The Shadow once said to the Body, "Who is a friend like me? I follow you wherever you go. In sunlight or in moonlight I never forsake you." "True," replied the Body. "You go with me in sunlight and in moonlight. But where are you when neither sun nor moon shines upon me?"

The most beautiful illustration of our theme, the faithful and unashamed friend, is the story of David and Jonathan. David was the natural and inevitable rival for the throne to Saul's son, Jonathan. Yet Jonathan "stripped himself" (1 Sam. 18:4) for the sake of David, and said to him, "Thou shalt be king over Israel, and I shall be next unto thee" (23:17). Although he risked his own life, he did not forsake David in the day of his adversity when he was pursued by the jealous rage of Saul. How pleasing is that incident in the wood of Ziph! David, pursued by Saul, was hiding with his companions in the forest of Ziph. From what follows, we know that he was beginning to lose heart, and his faith in God was shaken. That night Jonathan, with great peril to himself, left the lines of Saul's army and went over to David in the wood of Ziph, and there "strengthened his hand in God" (v. 16). That is the highest service one friend can do for another—strengthen his hand in God in the day of adversity. Jonathan was not ashamed of David's chain. No wonder that when he heard of Jonathan's death in battle on Mount Gilboa David exclaimed, "Thy love to me was wonderful, passing the love of women!" (2 Sam. 1:26).

The Friend Above All Friends

Onesiphorus was a faithful and unashamed friend to Paul because both of them were friends of the Friend who sticks closer than a brother. Not many of us can have a friend like Paul to whom to minister, and not many, either, in the dark hours of life can have a friend like Onesiphorus to minister to us. No, I take that back. We all have that greatest of all friends, the Friend of friends, the "Friend of sinners." That Friend is never ashamed of your chain. He is the one who never leaves and never forsakes you. "Greater love," said that Friend, "hath no man than this, that a man lay down his life for his friends" (John 15:13). And he who said that did that very thing. When we were lost and entangled in the wood and thicket of sin, He came to seek us and to strengthen our hand in God. Robert Robinson has stated this well in the following poem:

> Jesus sought me when a stranger,
> Wand'ring from the fold of God;
> He, to rescue me from danger,
> Interposed His precious blood.

Onesiphorus, true and faithful friend, not ashamed of Paul's chain, and who did seek and hunt for Paul there in ancient Rome until you had found him and had often refreshed him; the very mention of your name is like a cool, refreshing wind. Long since, we know, Paul's prayer for you has been answered, and you have found mercy before God. May we too find that same sweet mercy. Inspire our hearts, Onesiphorus, to be the loving, faithful friend to those in chains, even as you were to Paul. May we never be ashamed of our friends' chains, but ever refresh them, as you did for Paul in his dungeon there at Rome. O friend of Paul, O friend of Christ, will you now permit us to call you friend? And if, Onesiphorus, it be permitted to the souls in heaven to pray for those upon earth, then humbly we ask that as Paul prayed for you so you will pray for us that we too may obtain mercy in "that day."

Simon of Cyrene:
Up from the Country and Pressed into the Service

Charles Haddon Spurgeon (1834–1892) is undoubtedly the most famous minister of the nineteenth century. Converted in 1850, he united with the Baptists and soon began to preach in various places. He became pastor of the Baptist church in Waterbeach, England, in 1851, and three years later he was called to the decaying Park Street Church, London. Within a short time, the work began to prosper, a new church was built and dedicated in 1861, and Spurgeon became London's most popular preacher. In 1855, he began to publish his sermons weekly; today they make up the fifty-seven volumes of *The Metropolitan Tabernacle Pulpit*. He founded a pastor's college and several orphanages.

This sermon was taken from *The Metropolitan Tabernacle Pulpit*, volume 31.

12

Simon of Cyrene: Up from the Country and Pressed into the Service

And they compel one Simon a Cyrenian, who passed by, coming out of the country, the father of Alexander and Rufus, to bear his cross. (Mark 15:21)

JOHN TELLS US THAT our Savior went forth bearing His cross (see John 19:17). We are much indebted to John for inserting that fact. The other evangelists mention Simon the Cyrenian as bearing the cross of Christ. But John, who often fills up gaps that are left by the other three, tells us that Jesus set out to Calvary carrying His own cross. Our Lord Jesus came out from Pilate's palace laden with His cross. But He was so extremely emaciated, and so greatly worn by the night of the bloody sweat, that the procession moved too slowly for the rough soldiers. Therefore, they took the cross from their prisoner and laid it upon Simon. Or, possibly, they laid the long end upon the shoulder of the strong countryman while the Savior still continued to bear in part His cross until He came to the place of doom.

It is well that we should be told that the Savior bore His cross. For if it had not been so, objectors would have had ground for disputation. I hear them say, "You admit in the Old Testament that one of the most prominent types of the sacrifice of the Son of God was Abraham's offering up his son Isaac. Now Abraham laid the wood upon Isaac his son and not upon a servant. Should not, therefore, the Son of God bear the cross Himself?" Had not our Lord carried His cross, there would have been a flaw in His fulfillment of the type. Therefore, the Savior must bear the wood when He goes forth to be offered up as a sacrifice. One of the greatest of English preachers has well reminded us that the fulfillment of this type appeared to have been in eminent jeopardy, since, at the very first, our Lord's weakness must have been apparent, and the reason which led to the laying of the cross upon the Cyrenian might have prevented our Lord's carrying the cross at all. If the soldiers had a little earlier put the cross upon Simon, which they might very naturally have done, then the prophecy would not have been fulfilled. But God has the minds of men so entirely at His control, that even in the minutest circumstance He can order all things so as to complete the merest jots and tittles of the prophecy. Our Lord was made to be, in all points, an Isaac. Therefore we see him going forth bearing the wood of the burnt offering. Thus you see that it was important that Jesus should for a while bear His own cross.

But it was equally instructive that someone else should be made a partaker of the burden, for it has always been part of the divine counsel that for the salvation of men from sin the Lord should be associated with His church. So far as atonement is concerned, the Lord has trodden the winepress alone, and of the people there was none with Him. But as far as the conversion of the world is concerned, and its rescue from the power of error and wickedness, Christ is not alone. We are workers together with God. We are ourselves to be, in the hands of God, part bearers of the sorrow and travail by which men are to be delivered from the bondage of sin and Satan, and brought into the liberty of truth and righteousness. Hence, it became important that in the bearing of the cross, though not in the death upon it, there should be yoked with the Christ one who should follow close behind Him. To bear the cross after Jesus is the office of the faithful. Simon the Cyrenian is the representative of the whole church of God and of each believer in particular. Often had Jesus said, "Whosoever doth not bear his cross, and come after me, cannot be my disciple" (Luke 14:27). Now at last he embodies that sermon in an actual person. The disciple must be as his Master. He that would follow the crucified must himself bear the cross. This we see visibly set forth in Simon of Cyrene with the cross of Jesus laid upon his shoulder.

> Shall Simon bear the cross alone,
> And all the rest go free?
> No; there's a cross for every one,
> And there's a cross for me.

The lesson to each one of us is to take up our Lord's cross without delay and go with Him, without the camp, bearing His reproach. That many among this vast and mixed congregation may imitate Simon is the anxious desire of my heart. With holy expectancy I gaze upon this throng collected from all parts of the earth, and I long to find in it some who will take my Lord's yoke upon them this day.

Unexpected Persons Are Often Called to Crossbearing

I will begin with this first remark, that unexpected persons are often called to crossbearing. Like Simon, they are impressed into the service of Christ. Our text says, "They compel one Simon a Cyrenian, who passed by, coming out of the country, the father of Alexander and Rufus, to bear his cross." Simon did not volunteer but was forced into this work of crossbearing. It would seem from another evangelist that he speedily yielded to the impressment and lifted the burden heartily, but at first he was compelled. A rude authority was exercised by the guard, who being upon the governor's business acted with high-handed rigor, and forced whomsoever they pleased to do their bidding. By the exercise of such irresponsible power they compelled a passing stranger to carry Christ's cross. It was specially singular that the man to have this honor was not Peter, nor James, nor John, nor any one of the many who had for years listened to the Redeemer's speech; but it was a stranger from northern Africa who had been in no way connected with the life or teachings of Jesus of Nazareth.

Notice, first, that *he was an unknown man.* He was spoken of "as one Simon." Simon was a very common name among the Jews, almost as common as John in our own country. This man was just "one Simon"—an individual who need not be further described. But the providence of God had determined that this obscure individual, this certain man, or I might better say, this uncertain man, should be selected to the high office of crossbearer to the Son of God. I have an impression upon my mind that there is "one Simon" here this morning who has to bear Christ's cross from this time forward. I feel persuaded that I am right. That person is so far unknown that most probably he does not recognize a single individual in all this throng, neither does anybody in this assembly know anything of *him.* Certainly the preacher does not. He is one John, one Thomas, or one William. Perhaps, in the feminine, she is one Mary, one Jane, one Maggie. Friend, nobody knows you save our Father who is in heaven, and He has appointed you to have fellowship with His Son. I shall roughly describe you as "one Simon" and leave the Holy Spirit to bring you into your place and service.

But this "one Simon" was a very particular "*one* Simon." I lay the emphasis where there might seem to be no need of any. He was one whom God knew, chose, loved, and set apart for this special service. In a congregation like the present, there may be somebody whom our God intends to use for His glory during the rest of his life. That person sits in the pew and listens to what I am saying. Perhaps, as yet, he does not begin to inquire whether he is that "one Simon," that one person. Yet it is so, and before this sermon is ended, he shall know that the call to bear the cross is for him. Many more unlikely things than this have happened in this house of prayer. I pray that many a man may go out from this house a different man from the man he was when he entered it an hour ago.

That man Saul, that great persecutor of the church, afterward became such a mighty preacher of the gospel that people exclaimed with wonder, "There is a strange alteration in this man." "Why," said one, "when I knew him he was a Pharisee of the Pharisees. He was as bigoted a man as ever wore a phylactery, and he hated Christ and Christians so intensely that he could never persecute the church sufficiently." "Yes," replied another, "it was so. But he has had a strange twist. They say that he was going down to Damascus to hunt out the disciples, and something happened. We do not know exactly what it was, but evidently it gave him such a turn that he has never been himself since. In fact, he seems turned altogether upside down, and the current of his life is evidently reversed. He lives enthusiastically for that faith which once he destroyed." This speedy change happened to "one Saul of Tarsus." There were plenty of Sauls in Israel, but upon this one Saul electing love had looked in the counsels of eternity. For that Saul redeeming love had shed its heart's blood, and in that Saul effectual grace wrought mightily. Is there another Saul here today? The Lord grant that he may now cease to kick against the pricks, and may we soon hear of him, "Behold, he prayeth" (Acts 9:11). I feel convinced the counterpart of that "one Simon" is in this house at this moment. My prayer goes up to God, and I hope it is attended with the prayers of many thousands besides, that he may at once submit to the Lord Jesus.

It did not seem likely that Simon should bear the cross of Christ, for *he was a stranger who had newly come up from the country.* He probably knew little or nothing of what had been taking place in Jerusalem, for he had come from another continent. He was "one Simon a Cyrenian." I suppose that Cyrene could not have been less than eight hundred miles from

Jerusalem. It was situated in what is now called Tripoli in northern Africa, in which place a colony of Jews had been formed long before. Very likely he had come in a Roman galley from Alexandria to Joppa, and there had been rowed through the surf and landed in time to reach Jerusalem for the Passover. He had long wanted to come to Jerusalem. He had heard the fame of the temple and of the city of his fathers. He had longed to see the great assembly of the tribes and the solemn Paschal feast. He had traveled all those miles and had hardly yet got the motion of the ship out of his brain. It had never entered into his head that he would be impressed by the Roman guard and made to assist at an execution.

It was a singular providence that he should come into the city at the moment of the turmoil about Jesus and should have crossed the street just as the sad procession started on its way to Golgotha. He passed by neither too soon nor too late. He was on the spot as punctually as if he had made an appointment to be there. Yet, as men speak, it was all by mere chance. I cannot tell how many providences had worked together to bring him there in the nick of time, but so the Lord would have it and so it came about. He, a man there in Cyrene in northern Africa, must at a certain date, at the tick of the clock, be at Jerusalem in order that he might help to carry the cross up to Mount Calvary—*and he was there.* Ah! my dear friend, I do not know what providences have been at work to bring you here today—perhaps very strange ones. If a little something had occurred you would not have taken this journey. It only needed a small dust to turn the scale and you would have been hundreds of miles from this spot in quite another scene from this. Why you are here you do not yet know, except that you have come to listen to the preacher and join the throng. But God knows why He has brought you here. I trust it will be read in the annals of the future,

> Thus the eternal mandate ran,
> Almighty grace arrest that man.

God has brought you here that on this spot, by the preaching of the gospel, you may be compelled to bear the cross of Jesus. I pray it may be so. "One Simon a Cyrenian, coming out of the country," is here after a long journey, and this day he will begin to live a higher and a better life.

Further, notice, *Simon had come for another purpose.* He had journeyed to Jerusalem with no thought of bearing the cross of Jesus. Probably Simon was a Jew far removed from the land of his fathers. He had made a pilgrimage to the holy city to keep the Passover. Every Jew loved to be present at Jerusalem at the Paschal feast. So, to put it roughly, it was holiday time. It was a time for making an excursion to the capital. It was a season for making a journey and going up to the great city which was "beautiful for situation, the joy of the whole earth" (Ps. 48:2). Simon from far-off Cyrene must by all means keep the feast at Jerusalem. Perhaps he had saved his money for months that he might pay his fare to Joppa. He had counted down the gold freely for the joy that he had in going to the city of David and the temple of his God.

He was come for the Passover and for that only. He would be perfectly satisfied to go home when once the feast was over, and once he had partaken of the lamb with the tribes of Israel. Then he could say throughout the rest of his life, "I, too, was once at the great feast of our people when we commemorated the coming up out of Egypt." Friends, we propose one way, but God has other propositions. We say, "I will step in and hear the preacher," but God means that the arrows of His grace shall stick fast in our hearts. Many and many a time with no desire for grace men have listened to the gospel, and the Lord has been found of them that sought Him not. I heard of one who cared little for the sermon until the preacher chanced to use that word "eternity," and the hearer was taken prisoner by holy thoughts and led to the Savior's feet. Men have stepped into places of worship even with evil designs, and yet the purpose of grace has been accomplished. They came to scoff, but they remained to pray. Some have been cast by the providence of

God into positions where they have met with Christian men, and a word of admonition has been blessed to them.

A lady was one day at an evening party, and there met with Caesar Malan, the famous divine of Geneva, who, in his usual manner, inquired of her whether she was a Christian. She was startled, surprised, and vexed and made a short reply to the effect that it was not a question she cared to discuss. Whereupon, Mr. Malan replied with great sweetness that he would not persist in *speaking* of it, but he would pray that she might be led to give her heart to Christ and become a useful worker for Him. Within a fortnight she met the minister again and asked him how she must come to Jesus. Mr. Malan's reply was, "Come to Him just as you are." That lady gave herself up to Jesus. It was Charlotte Elliott, to whom we owe that precious hymn:

> Just as I am—without one plea
> But that thy blood was shed for me,
> And that thou bidd'st me come to thee—
> O Lamb of God, I come.

It was a blessed thing for her that she was at that party, and that the servant of God from Geneva had been there and had spoken to her so faithfully. Oh for many a repetition of the story "of one Simon a Cyrenian," coming, not with the intent to bear the cross, but with quite another mind, and yet being enlisted in the crossbearing army of the Lord Jesus!

I would have you notice, once more, that this man was at this particular time not thinking upon the subject at all, for *he was at that time merely passing by.* He had come up to Jerusalem, and whatever occupied his mind he does not appear to have taken any notice of the trial of Jesus or of the sad end of it. It is expressly said that he "passed by." He was not even sufficiently interested in the matter to stand in the crowd and look at the mournful procession. Women were weeping there right bitterly—the daughters of Jerusalem to whom the Master said, "Weep not for me, but weep for yourselves, and for your children" (Luke 23:28). But this man passed by. He was anxious to hurry away from so unpleasant a sight and to get up to the temple. He was quietly making his way through the crowd, eager to go about his business. He must have been greatly surprised and distressed when a rough hand was laid upon him and a stern voice said, "Shoulder that cross." There was no resisting a Roman centurion when he gave a command, and so the countryman meekly submitted, wishing, no doubt, that he were back in Cyrene tilling the ground. He must needs stoop his shoulder and take up a new burden and tread in the footsteps of the mysterious personage to whom the cross belonged. He was only passing by, and yet he was enlisted and impressed by the Romans—as I take it, impressed by the grace of God for life. For whereas Mark says he was the father of Alexander and Rufus, it would seem that his sons were well known to the Christian people to whom Mark was writing. If his son was the same Rufus that Paul mentions, then he greets him saying, "Salute Rufus . . . his mother and mine" (Rom. 16:13). It would seem that Simon's wife and his sons became believers and partakers of the sufferings of Christ. His contact with the Lord in that strange compulsory way probably wrought out for him another and more spiritual contact that made him a true crossbearer.

All you that pass by this day, draw near to Jesus! I have no wish to call your attention to myself, far from it. But I do ask your attention to my Lord. Though you only intended to slip into this tabernacle and slip out again, I pray that you may be arrested by a call from my Lord. I speak as my Lord's servant, and I would constrain you to come to Him. Stand where you are awhile and let me beg you to yield to His love, which even now would cast the bands of a man around you. I would compel you, by my Lord's authority, to take up His cross and bear it after Him. It would be strange, you say. So it might be, but it would be a glorious event. I remember Mr. Knill, speaking of his own conversion, used an expression that I would like to use concerning one of you. Here it is: "It was just a quarter past twelve, August 2, when twang went every harp in paradise, for a sinner had repented." May it be so with you. Oh that every harp in paradise may now ring out the high praises of sovereign grace as you now yield yourself to the great Shepherd and Bishop of souls! May that divine impressment which is imaged in the text by the compulsion of the Roman soldier take place in your case at this very moment. May it be seen in your instance that unexpected persons are often called to be crossbearers!

Crossbearing Can Still Be Practiced

My second observation is *crossbearing can still be practiced*. Very briefly let me tell you in what ways the cross can still be carried.

First, and chiefly, *by your becoming a Christian*. If the cross shall take you up, you will take up the cross. Christ will be your hope, His death your trust, Himself the object of your love. You never become a crossbearer truly until you lay your burdens down at His feet who bore the cross and curse for you.

Next, you become a crossbearer *when you make an open avowal of the Lord Jesus Christ*. Do not deceive yourselves—this is expected of each one of you if you are to be saved. The promise as I read it in the New Testament is not to the believer alone but to the believer who confesses his faith. "For with the heart man believeth unto righteousness; and with the mouth confession is made unto salvation" (Rom. 10:10). He says, "Whosoever therefore shall confess me before men, him will I confess also before my Father which is in heaven. But whosoever shall deny me before men"—and from the connection it should seem to mean, he that does not confess Me—"him will I also deny before my Father which is in heaven" (Matt. 10:32–33). To quote the inspired Scripture, "He that believeth and is baptized shall be saved" (Mark 16:16). There should be, there must be, the open avowal in Christ's own way of the secret faith that you have in Him.

Now this is often a cross. Many people would like to go to heaven by an underground railway—secrecy suits them. They do not want to cross the channel. The sea is too rough. But when there is a tunnel made they will go to the fair country. My good people, you are cowardly, and I must quote to you a text that ought to sting your cowardice out of you: "But the fearful, and unbelieving . . . shall have their part in the lake which burneth with fire and brimstone" (Rev. 21:8). I say no more and make no personal applications. But, I beseech you, run no risks. Be afraid to be afraid. Be ashamed of being ashamed of Christ. Shame on that man who counts it any shame to say before assembled angels and men and devils, "I am a follower of Christ." May you who have hitherto been secret followers of the crucified Lord become manifest crossbearers! Do you not even now cry out, "Set down my name, sir"?

Further, some have to take up their cross by *commencing Christian work*. You live in a village where there is no gospel preaching, preach yourself. You are in a backwoods town where the preaching is very far from being such as God approves of, begin to preach the truth yourself. "Alas!" you say, "I would make a fool of myself." Are you ashamed to be a fool for Christ? "Oh, but I would break down." Break down, it will do you good. Perhaps you may break somebody else down. There is no better preaching in the world than that of a man who breaks down under a sense of unworthiness. If that breakdown communicates itself to other people, it may begin a revival. If you are choked by your earnestness, others may become earnest too. Do you still murmur, "But I would get the ill will of everybody"? For Christ's sake could you not bear that? When the good monk said to Martin Luther, "Go thou home to thy cell and keep quiet," why did Martin not take the advice? Why, indeed? "It is very bad for young people to be so forward. You will do a great deal of mischief; therefore, be quiet, you Martin. Who are you to interfere with the great authorities? Be holy for yourself and don't trouble others. If you stir up a reformation, thousands of good people will be burned through you. Do be quiet." Bless God, Martin did not go home, and he was not quiet, but went about his Master's business and raised heaven and earth by his brave witness bearing. Where are you, Martin, this morning? I pray God to call you out. As you have confessed His name and are His servant, I pray that He may make you bear public testimony for Him and tell out the saving power of the Savior's precious blood. Come, Simon, I see you shrink. But the cross has to be carried; therefore, bow your back. It is only a wooden cross, after all, and not an iron one. You can bear it. You must bear it. God help you.

Perhaps, too, some brother may have to take up his cross by *bearing witness against the rampant sin that surrounds him.* "Leave all those dirty matters alone. Do not say a word about them. Let the people go to the Devil or else you will soil your white kid gloves." Sirs, we will spoil our hands as well as our gloves. We will risk our characters if need be, but we will put down the devilry that now defiles London. Truly the flesh does shrink, and the purest part of our manhood shrinks with it, when we are compelled to bear open protest against sins that are done of men in secret. But, Simon, the Master may yet compel you to bear His cross in this respect, and if so, He will give you both courage and wisdom. Your labor shall not be in vain in the Lord.

Sometimes, however, the crossbearing is of another and more quiet kind and may be described as *submission to providence.* A young friend is saying, "For me to live at home I know to be my duty. But father is unkind, and the family generally impose upon me. I wish I could get away." Ah! dear sister, you must bear Christ's cross, and it may be the Lord would have you remain at home. Therefore bear the cross. A servant is saying, "I would like to be in a Christian family. I do not think I can stop where I am." Perhaps, good sister, the Lord has put you where you are to be a light in a dark place. All the lamps should not be in one street or what will become of the courts and alleys? It is often the duty of a Christian man to say, "I will stop where I am and fight this matter through. I mean by character and example, with kindness and courtesy and love, to win this place for Jesus." Of course, the easy way is to turn monk and live quietly in a cloister and serve God by doing nothing.

Or you can turn nun and dwell in a convent and expect to win the battle of life by running out of it. Is not this absurd? If you shut yourself away from this poor world, what is to become of it? You men and women that are Christians must stand up and stand out for Jesus where the providence of God has cast you. If your calling is not a sinful one, and if the temptations around you are not too great for you, you must "hold the fort" and never dream of surrender. If your lot is hard, look upon it as Christ's cross, and bow your back to the load. Your shoulder may be raw at first, but you will grow stronger before long, for as your day your strength shall be. "It is good for a man that he bear the yoke in his youth" (Lam. 3:27). But it is good for a man to bear the cross in his old age as well as in his youth. In fact, we ought never to quit so blessed a burden. What wings are to a bird and sails to a ship, that the cross becomes to a man's spirit when he fully consents to accept it as his life's beloved load. Truly did Jesus say, "My yoke is easy, and my burden is light" (Matt. 11:30). Now, Simon, where are you? Shoulder the cross, man, in the name of God!

To Crossbearing There Are Noble Compulsions

Thirdly, to crossbearing there are noble compulsions. Simon's compulsion was the rough hand of the Roman legionary and the gruff voice in the Latin tongue, "Shoulder that cross." But we hear gentler voices that compel us this day to take up Christ's cross.

The first compulsion is this: *"The love of Christ constraineth us"* (2 Cor. 5:14). He has done all this for you; therefore, by sweet but irresistible compulsion, you are made to render Him some return of love. Does not Jesus appear to you in a vision as you sit in this house? Do you not see that thorn-crowned head, that visage crimsoned with the bloody sweat, those hands and feet pierced with the nails? Does He not say to you pointedly, "I did all this for you. What have you done for Me?" Startled in your seat, you cover your face and inwardly reply, "I will answer that question by the rest of my life. I will be first and foremost a servant of Jesus. I will not be a trader first and a Christian next, but a Christian first and a businessman afterward." You, my sister, must say, "I will live for Christ as a daughter, a wife, or a mother. I will live for my Lord, for He has given Himself for me. I am not my own, but bought with a price."

The true heart will feel a compulsion arising from a second reflection, namely, *the glory of a life spent for God and for His Christ.* What is the life of a man who toils in business, makes money, becomes rich, and dies? It winds up with a paragraph in the *Illustrated London News* declaring that he died worth so much. The wretch was not worth anything himself. His estate had value, he had none. Had he been worth anything he would have sent his money about the world doing good. But as a worthless steward he laid his Master's stores in heaps to rot. The life of multitudes of men is self-seeking. It is ill for a man to live the life of swine. What a poor creature is the usual ordinary man! But a life spent for Jesus, though it involve crossbearing, is noble, heroic, and sublime. The mere earthworm leads a dunghill life. A life of what is called pleasure is a mean, beggarly business. A life of keeping up respectability is utter slavery. A life wholly consecrated to Christ and His cross is life indeed. It is akin to the life of angels. Higher still, it is the life of God within the soul of man. All you that have a spark of true nobility, seek to live lives worth living, worth remembering, worthy to be the commencement of eternal life before the throne of God.

Some of you ought to feel the cross coming upon your shoulders this morning when you think of *the needs of those among whom you live.* They are dying, perishing for lack of knowledge, rich and poor alike, ignorant of Christ. Multitudes of them are wrapped up in self-righteousness. They are perishing, and those who ought to warn them are often dumb dogs that cannot bark. Do you not feel that you ought to deliver the sheep from the wolf? Have you no bowels of compassion? Are your hearts turned to steel? I am sure you cannot deny that the times demand of you earnest and forceful lives. No Christian man can now sit still without incurring awful guilt. Whether you live in London or in any other great town amid reeking sin, or dwell in the country amid the dense darkness that broods over many rural districts, you are under bonds to be up and doing. It may be a cross to you, but for Jesus' sake you must uplift it and never lay it down until the Lord calls you home.

Some of you should bear the cross of Christ *because the cause of Christ is at a discount where you dwell.* I delight in a man in whom the lordlier chivalry has found a congenial home. He loves to espouse the cause of truth in the cloudy and dark day. He never counts heads but weighs arguments. When he settles down in a town he never inquires, "Where is the most respectable congregation? Where can I meet with those who will give me the best advantage in business?" No, he studies his conscience rather than his convenience. He hears one say, "There is a nonconformist chapel, but it is down a back street. There is a Baptist church, but the members are nearly all poor, and no gentlefolk are among them. Even the evangelical church is down at the heel. The best families attend the high church." I say he hears this, and his heart is sick of such talk. He will go where the gospel is preached and nowhere else. Fine architecture has scant charms for him, and grand music is no part of his religion. If these are substitutes for the gospel, he abhors them. It is meanness itself for a man to forsake the truth for the sake of respectability. Multitudes who ought to be found maintaining the good old cause are recreant to their convictions, if indeed they ever had any. For this cause the true man resolves to stick to truth through thick and thin, and not to forsake her because her adherents are poor and despised. If ever we might temporize, that time is past and gone.

I arrest yonder man this morning, who has long been a Christian, but has concealed half his Christianity in order to be thought respectable or to escape the penalties of faithfulness. Come out from those with whom you are numbered, but with whom you are not united in heart. Be brave enough to defend a good cause against all comers. The day shall come when he shall have honor for his reward who accepted dishonor that he might be true to his God, his Bible, and his conscience. Blessed be he that can be loyal to his Lord, cost him what it may—loyal even in those matters which traitors call little things. We would compel that Simon the Cyrenian this day bear the cross because there are so few to bear it in these degenerate days.

Besides, I may say to some of you, you ought to bear the cross because you know you are not satisfied. *Your hearts are not at rest.* You have prospered in worldly things, but you are not happy. You have good health, but you are not happy. You have loving friends, but you are not happy. There is but one way of getting rest to the heart, and that is, to come to Jesus. That is His word: "Come unto me, all ye that labor and are heavy laden, and I will give you rest" (Matt. 11:28). If after this you need a further rest for other and higher longings, then you must come again to the same Savior and hearken to His next word: "Take my yoke upon you, and learn of me; for I am meek and lowly in heart: and ye shall find rest unto your souls. For my yoke is easy, and my burden is light" (v. 29–30). Some of you professors have not yet found perfect rest, and the reason is because you have looked to the cross for pardon, but have never taken to crossbearing as an occupation. You are hoping *in* Christ but not living *for* Christ. The finding of rest to your soul will come to you in having something to do or to bear for Jesus. "Take my yoke upon you . . . and ye shall find rest unto your souls."

There are many ways, then, of bearing the cross for Christ, and there are many reasons why some here present should begin at once to carry the load.

Crossbearing Is a Blessed Occupation

To close, bear with me a minute or two while I say that crossbearing is a blessed occupation. I feel sure that Simon found it so. Let me mention certain blessings that must have attended the special service of Simon. First, *it brought him into Christ's company*. When they compelled him to bear His cross, he was brought close to Jesus. If it had not been for that compulsion he might have gone his way or might have been lost in the crowd. But now he is in the inner circle near to Jesus. For the first time in his life he saw that blessed form, and as he saw it I believe his heart was enamored with it. As they lifted the cross on his shoulders he looked at that sacred person and saw a crown of thorns about His brow. As he looked at his fellow sufferer, he saw all down His cheeks the marks of bloody sweat and black and blue bruises from cruel hands. As for those eyes, they looked him through and through! That face, that matchless face, he had never seen its like. Majesty was therein blended with misery, innocence with agony, and love with sorrow. He would never have seen that countenance so well nor marked the whole form of the Son of Man so dearly if he had not been called to bear that cross. It is wonderful how much we see of Jesus when we suffer or labor for Him. Believing souls, I pray that this day you may be so impressed into my Lord's service that you may have nearer and dearer fellowship with Him than in the past. If any man will do His will, he shall know of the doctrine. They see Jesus best who carry His cross most.

Besides, *the cross held Simon in Christ's steps*. Do you catch it? If Jesus carried the front part of the cross and Simon followed behind, he was sure to put his feet down just where the Master's feet had been before. The cross is a wonderful implement for keeping us in the way of our Lord. As I was turning this subject over, I was thinking how often I had felt a conscious contact between myself and my Lord when I have had to bear reproach for His sake. At the same time, I have been led to watch my steps more carefully because of that very reproach. Friends, we do not want to slip from under the cross. If we did so, we might slip away from our Lord and from holy walking. If we can keep our shoulder beneath that sacred load and see our Lord a little on before, we shall be making the surest progress. This being near to Jesus is a blessed privilege, which is cheaply purchased at the price of crossbearing. If you would see Jesus, bestir yourselves to work for Him. Boldly avow Him, cheerfully suffer for Him, and then you shall see Him and shall learn to follow Him step by step. O blessed cross, which holds us to Jesus and to His ways!

Then Simon had this honor, that *he was linked with Christ's work.* He could not put away sin, but he could assist weakness. Simon did not die on the cross to make expiation, but he did live under the cross to aid in the accomplishment of the divine purpose. You and I cannot interfere with Jesus in His passion, but we can share with Him in His compassion. We cannot purchase liberty for the enslaved, but we can tell them of their emancipation. To have a finger in Christ's work is glory. I invite the man that seeks honor and immortality to seek it thus. To have a share in the Redeemer's work is a more attractive thing than all the pomp and glitter of this world and the kingdoms thereof. Where are the men of heavenly mind who will covet to be joined to the Lord in this ministry? Let them step out and say, "Jesus, I my cross have taken. Henceforth I will follow You. Come life or death, I will carry Your cross until You shall give me the crown."

While Simon was carrying the cross through the crowd, I doubt not that the rough soldiery would deal him many a kick or buffet, but I feel equally sure that the dear Master sometimes stole a glance at him. *Simon enjoyed Christ's smile.* I know the Lord so well, that I feel sure He must have done so. He would not forget the man who was His partner for the while. And oh, that look! How Simon must have treasured up the remembrance of it. "I never carried a load that was so light," says he, "as that which I carried that morning. For when the Blessed One smiled at me amid His woes, I felt myself to be strong as Hercules." Alexander, his firstborn, and that redheaded lad Rufus when they grew up both felt it to be the honor of the family that their father carried the cross after Jesus. Rufus and Alexander had a patent of nobility in being the sons of such a man. Mark recorded the fact that Simon carried the cross, and that such and such persons were his sons. I think when the old man came to lie upon his deathbed he said, "My hope is in Him whose cross I carried. Blessed burden lay me down in my grave. This body of mine cannot perish, for it bore the cross that Jesus carried and that carried *Him*. I shall rise again to see Him in His glory, for His cross has pressed me, and His love will surely raise me." Happy are we if we can, while yet we live, be coworkers together with Him, that when He comes in His kingdom we may be partakers of His glory. "Blessed is the man that endureth temptation: for when he is tried, he shall receive the crown of life, which the Lord hath promised to them that love him" (James 1:12). God bless you, and especially you who have come out of the country. God bless you. Amen and amen.